Barcode are pi
AE

CH00717696

The Brasses of Huntingdonshire

The Brasses of Huntingdonshire

Peter Heseltine

Cambridgeshire
Libraries
Publications

ISBN: 09024 36392
© **Peter Heseltine**   4 |88
First Published in 1987 by
Cambridgeshire Libraries Publications
c/o Central Library, Broadway,
Peterborough PE1 1RX
Telephone (0733) 48343

Printed by Cambridge Free Press Workers'
Co-operative, Gwydir Street, Cambridge.

Cover illustration: detail of a brass in Diddington Church.

INTRODUCTION

Huntingdonshire, when it existed as a separate administrative unit, was one of the smaller of the English counties. It has been joined with Cambridgeshire, to which has been added the Soke of Peterborough and parts of Northamptonshire. The county remains, in antiquarian and archaeological terms, an identifiable unit so it is reasonable to draw together an account of the pre-1750 brasses of the county.

All churches which are, or have been, part of Huntingdonshire are included as is the portion in the north of the new county, once the Soke of Peterborough, more usually identified as Northamptonshire. As these churches are now in Cambridgeshire they may be missed from any Northamptonshire listing. Four churches listed under Bedfordshire are included for similar reasons.

As in all counties, knowledge of the lost brasses substantially alters our understanding of what exists today. It has been estimated that as few as 10% remains of the brasses originally laid down. In Huntingdonshire the proportion of lost brasses may be higher due to the influence and depredations of the Puritans in the county of Cromwell. The Protector's visit to Peterborough Cathedral is recorded by Gunton in graphic detail. Not including the Cathedral, the known losses in the county are about 80%. In Bedfordshire, it is suggested by Jerome Bertram that the losses are less than 65% although further research will increase this figure substantially.

Traces of these lost brasses can be found. In the churches remain the evidence of indents. The published surveys of Bridges and Macklin identify many indents subsequently lost and through the private papers of antiquaries such as Astry, Stukeley and Gough, more records of lost brasses come to light.

Indeed, the modern study of brasses is like a detective story - the piecing together of evidence from many sources to build a complete picture.

Just how the brasses of the county have disappeared can be seen in this chart (Peterborough Cathedral and Museum are not included):

	Brasses	Lost	Total
Inscriptions	25	40	65
Figures	12	58	70
Pre-1350 brasses		21	21
Miscellaneous	2	14	16
	39	133	172
Possible brasses			14

1

THE SURVIVING BRASSES

It cannot be said that the surviving brasses are an outstanding collection, but the quality and interest of what remains is high.

There are good, if mechanical, designs at Sawtry where the brasses of Sir William and Lady de Moigne are the county's earliest existing figures. Those at Diddington and Marholm are more interesting than may appear at first. Tilbrook has an outstandingly artistic brass, now unfortunately covered by the organ. All of these are London engraved memorials. These are noted as Series, for example "B" or "D", which identifies the workshop to which they are allocated currently. The small priest at Somersham was probably made at Bury St Edmunds and the indents at Alconbury contained Cambridge engraved brasses. Some of the later figures and inscriptions, such as those at Stilton, are from the Southwark workshop of Bernard Johnson and Nicholas Stone.

There are a surprising number of pre-1350 indents partially reflecting the wealth of the area prior to the Black Death. The indents and brasses of Peterborough Cathedral, of which good drawings survive, are a marvellous collection. The Cathedral boasts a Royal brass to Catherine of Aragon, although it is a particularly miserable piece of metal and probably not contemporary.

The number after each extant brass (M.S.I) refers to its position in Mill Stephenson's list of brasses and serves as a useful shorthand identification.

PRINTED AND MANUSCRIPT SOURCES

Many of the early antiquaries recorded what they saw in the churches. The earliest, whose notes remain unpublished and are more usually know as the Cotton Manuscript, was Richard Astry. Born at Toseland about 1631, he went to Queens College, Cambridge and was elected an Alderman of Huntingdon. His notes are in the British Library. Other helpful visitors were Dugdale (Peterborough Cathedral), Richard Gough, whose notes are in the Bodleian and William Cole, better known for his Cambridgeshire notes, but useful on individual churches all over the country.

Two printed surveys have been of great assistance - one by a former Rector of Somersham, the Rev. Herbert Macklin, whose records of the county appear in the Transactions of the Monumental Brass Society and the other by the Royal Commission on Historical Monuments.

The Norris Library and Museum at St Ives has been very helpful, partly through the Inskip Ladds Collection, but also through a manuscript known as Clements Church Notes c1731, now probably lost, and the notebooks of John Cole.

ACKNOWLEDGEMENTS

For assistance with this paper I am grateful to:

Bedford Central Library
Bedfordshire Record Office
Bodleian Library
British Library, Manuscripts Department
Cambridgeshire County Library Service, Huntingdon branch
County Record Office, Huntingdon
Monumental Brass Society
Museum of Archaeology and Ethnology, Cambridge
National Art Library, Victoria and Albert Museum
Norris Library and Museum, St Ives
Northamptonshire Record Office
Society of Antiquaries
University Library of Cambridge

I am indebted to: the late Dr H.K.Cameron and Miss M.Cra'ster for access to the Cambridge Collection, Father Jerome Bertram for miscellaneous information, Dr John Blair for enquiries at the Bodleian Library.

Unless otherwise indicated the illustrations are by kind permission of the clergy and parochial church councils of the county. Conington church is now in the care of the Redundant Churches Fund.

The illustrations of Peterborough Cathedral are by kind permission of the Dean and Chapter; the lost brasses of the Cathedral by kind permission of the Trustees of the Winchelsea Estate; the brasses at Peterborough Museum by kind permission of Peterborough City Council.

For permission to reproduce rubbings from their collections, I am grateful to the Museum of Archaeology and Ethnology, Cambridge; the Society of Antiquaries, London; and Department of Antiquities, Ashmolean Museum, Oxford.

Other illustrations by kind permission of the Monumental Brass Society; Norris Library and Museum; County Record Office, Huntingdon and the Huntingdonshire Local History Society.

PICTURE SOURCES

Abbots Ripton: Cambridge Collection
Alconbury: Transactions of the Monumental Brass Society; photograph by author
Barnack: author
Broughton: photographs by author; remainder from Cambridge Collection
Buckden: author

3

Buckworth: Norris Library and Museum
Bythorne: photograph by author; rubbing from Transactions of the Monumental Brass Society
Colne: author
Conington: drawing from Victoria County History; photograph by author
Diddington: rubbings by author; drawing from Camden Society
Eaton Socon: photographs by author; drawing from Fisher.
Elton: author
Eynesbury: drawing from Norris Library and Museum
Fenstanton: author
Godmanchester: Cambridge Collection
Great Gransden: rubbing by author; photograph and plan from County Record Office, Huntingdon
Great Staughton: drawing from Camden Society
Great Stukeley: photograph by author; drawing from Bodleian Library
Helpston: author
Hemingford Abbots: author
Huntingdon All Saints: Cambridge Collection
Keystone: author
Leighton Bromswold: author
Little Gidding: palimpsest by David Cozens and Records of Huntingdonshire; rubbings from The Genealogist
Little Stukeley: author
Long Stow (or Stow Longa): author
Marholm: photographs by author; remainder from Transactions of the Monumental Brass Society
Maxey: author
Molesworth: photographs by author; drawings from Norris Library and Museum
Orton Waterville: Cambridge Collection
Peterborough Cathedral: photographs by author; rubbing from Oxford University Brass Rubbing Society Transactions; drawings from British Library
Peterborough Museum: author
St Neots: smaller illustration from Gough; other from Cutts
Sawtry: photograph from County Record Office, Huntingdon; and author ; drawing from the Bodleian Library
Somersham: rubbing from Cambridge Collection; photographs by author
Stanground: author
Steeple Gidding: author
Stibbington: author
Stilton: Cambridge Collection
Tilbrook: rubbing from Portfolio of the Monumental Brass Society; photograph by author
Thornhaugh: author
Ufford: author
Upwood: author
Winwick: author
Wyton: Norris Library and Museum

ABBOTS RIPTON

1. INSCRIPTION, THOMAS COWCHE, 1641, MURAL, VESTRY, (M.S.I).

An inscription plate, probably engraved at Southwark, and noted by Clements near the altar, reading:

THOMAS COWCHE GENT : WAS / BAPTIZED JANUARYE THE 26 /   1583
AND HIS BODY LYETH HERE / INTERRED WHO DEPARTED THIS /   LIFE
UPPON THE 20 DAY OF / FEBRUARY 1641 AETATIS SUAE 58.

ALCONBURY

1. INDENT OF CIVILIAN, WIFE, FOOT INSCRIPTION, c1520, NAVE.

A slab in the centre of the Nave showing a civilian and his wife, both in long gowns with the lady wearing a form of mob cap. This helps to identify it as a Cambridge School brass, probably engraved in the city. A note in the Norris Library and Museum says the original site of the slab was in the large pew near the easterly semi-pillar of the South Aisle and then in the Chancel near the pulpit.

2. DEDICATION PLATE, 1877.

Although a relatively modern brass, it is worth recording as it notes how the lower part of the tower was rebuilt while the bell-chamber and spire were supported by beams.

BARNACK

1. TWO BRASS SHIELDS, c1540.

These two shields have a chequered history and are fortunate to have survived. When the thatch was removed from a local cottage in the 1930's, the shield with the single coat was found. This bears:

Turner: Ermines, on a cross quarter-pierced argent, four fers-de-moline sable.

The thatch was burnt in a field and the ashes ploughed in. When the field was re-ploughed the following year, the second shield was discovered. It shows traces of the fire as most of the white metal has melted away. It bears:

Turner impaling **Sharpe:** Argent, three bird's heads (crows?) sable, beaked gules, a bordure engrailed azure, bezanty.

Among the PCC wills at Somerset House is that of John Turnor of Walcote, proved on November 27th, 1541. He requested his body "to be buryed ain the churche of Barnack aforesayd within Our Lady Chappel on the south syde of the high quere in a vaulte at the north ende of of the Aulter of the sayde chapell".

2.   INDENT OF FLORIATED CROSS, MARGINAL INSCRIPTION,   c1530, CHANCEL.

Now worn.

3.   INDENT OF LARGE FIGURE,   SINGLE CANOPY,   TWO SHIELDS, MARGINAL INSCRIPTION.

This indent of a particularly fine brass is next to No.2. The side shafts probably once bore figures. The slab has been cut at the top and the upper part of the canopy lost.

4.   INDENT OF KNEELING FIGURE,   SCROLL,   RELIGIOUS SYMBOL, INSCRIPTION, LADY CHAPEL.

This indent on the back of an Altar Tomb shows the figure of a man in armour.

5.   UNIDENTIFIED INDENT.

Dickinson in 1968 noted a large stone slab in the Nave which formerly bore a brass of which part of the indent was visible.

6.   LOST INDENTS.

Bridges noted the following indents, some of which may be a confusion with those remaining:

a.   Mural monument (No.4?): portrait, arms and inscription lost
b.   Man, wife, children, inscription lost (The figures may have remained) c.   A marginal inscription (No.2?) d.   Several indents.

BLUNTISHAM

1.   INDENT OF CIVILIAN, WIFE, INSCRIPTION, c1460, NAVE.

Now very worn, only the figure of a man in civil dress can be clearly distinguished.   It portrayed a civilian in a long tunic.

2.   INDENT OF RECTANGULAR PLATE, INSCRIPTION, NAVE.

This worn indent shows a rectangular plate - probably bearing an achievement - and an inscription beneath.

3.   INDENT OF INSCRIPTION, NAVE.

A simple inscription plate.

BROUGHTON

1. LAWRENCE MARTIN, IN CIVIL DRESS, FEET AND UPPER PART OF BODY LOST; WIFE, AGNES, PORTIONS OF MARGINAL INSCRIPTION, TWO SHIELDS, EMBLEMS LOST, c1490, NAVE, (M.S.I).

This is a Suffolk series brass, probably engraved in Bury St Edmunds. The Martin family were based around Long Melford, where they have other brasses, which may explain the Suffolk connection. All the portions of brass of which rubbings exist were loose in the Rectory prior to 1864. Some parts have not been seen since 1900 and could exist locally. These parts are:

a. One shield with the initials LM above a tun b. The evangelical symbol of St Luke c. Portions of the marginal inscription.

The illustration of the shield comes from the Cambridge Collection and the missing portions of the inscription from the collection of the Society of Antiquaries.

The marginal inscription reads (portion in brackets lost, remainder fixed to a pew):

   (f)...bonys...lyeht..here...(the)whych..augnes...Lawrence... decissid ...(in)...

The remaining part of the figure shows a man in a long, fur-lined gown with a gypciere (purse) and a scarf or hat. The indent of the wife shows a lady in a long gown and a pronounced pedimental head-dress with the lappets turned up.

2. INDENT OF ECCLESIASTIC WITH SCROLL AND CIVILIAN UNDER DOUBLE CANOPY, FOOT INSCRIPTION, FOUR ROUNDELS, c1450, NAVE.

This very fine indent in the Nave probably commemorates two brothers, one of whom could have been a Benedictine monk due to the connections between Broughton and Ramsey Abbey.

3. INDENT OF CIVILIAN, WIFE, FOOT INSCRIPTION, c1460?, NAVE.

This slab is now badly worn and broken and the indents difficult to identify.

BUCKDEN

1. INSCRIPTION, SARAH REYNOLDS, 1726, CHANCEL.

This simple oval brass reads:

   SARAH DAUGHTER / OF DR GEORGE REYNOLDS / OCTR.19.1726.

2. THREE BRASSES.

Three other brasses probably remain under the fixed carpet. They read:

a. RICHARD SON OF / ANTO. REYNOLDS ESQR / JANUARY THE 3RD 1737

b. THE HONBLE / ANNA SOPHIA REYNOLDS / AUGUST YE 20 1737

c. THE HONBLE SARAH REYNOLDS / WIFE OF RCH LD BP OF LINCOLN / APR 7 1740

3. INDENT, NOW LOST.

Clements records "under a large grey marble slab near the Chancel entrance (whose brasses are now torn off) are buried Charles Brandon and his brother Henry, both Dukes of Suffolk who died at Buckden on the same day (and were buried in one grave) of the sweating sickness, July 14th 1551". The Church Guide refers to a table tomb to the two Dukes in the churchyard. These lines are preserved by Camden:

Una fides vivos conjunxit, religio una; / Ardor et in studiis unus et unus amor / Abstulit hos simul una dies: duo corpora jungit / Una urna de mentos unus Olympus habet

BUCKWORTH

1. CROSS, FIGURE, FOUR SHIELDS, LOMBARDIC MARGINAL INSCRIPTION, NOW LOST.

In the Norris Collection of Engravings is a drawing from Mrs J.H. Parker's Scrapbook of Coffin Lids which shows a curious cross rising from a niche in which is a figure, possibly the Blessed Virgin Mary, and four shields between the arms of the cross. This may have been copied from a drawing in Gough. The inscription reads:

VOUS : QUI : PAR : ICI : PASSEZ : PUR : LALME : ....M : URMAE : VARROTE : MERCI : LUI : PACE

2. INSCRIPTION, ROBERT PEELE, 1637, NOW LOST.

In the Norris Library and Museum a manuscript by John Cole notes this on a brass in the Chancel:

Here lyeth buried the body of Robert Peele of this Parrish Gent who departed this life the 9th day of May A 1637 aged 77 yeares and three months. Vivit post funera virtus.

Reader if faire thouldst learne who heer is shrind / Ask all these neighbouringe parts and thou shalt find / This was a grave wise liver whose chast dust / Jme chosen treasurer to keepe in trust / Ask all that knew him Theyle mouch the same / Good was his life his death and now his fame.

3.   THREE CROSSES WITH LOMBARDIC INSCRIPTIONS,   NOW LOST.

The College of Arms, Brooke Collection, contains a reference to three inscriptions in Saxon letters, brass crosses gone, in Buckworth Chancel.   One of these may be No.1.

BYTHORNE

1.   INSCRIPTION, SILLINA PARRIS, 1659, NAVE, (M.S.I).

A small inscription which reads:

HERE   LYETH YE BODY OF / SILLINA PARRIS YE WIFE / OF   WILLIAM PARRIS SHEE / DYED YE 31TH OF OCTOB 1658.

2.   INSCRIPTION 1660.

A brass to an unknown man whose name may been cut on the stone.   It reads:

Here lyes one whom God did call to lend / his latter days in teaching in this place / This little vynyard he strove to defend / from all that might it harme or else deface / Whatever men may deem he finds his paines / now recompensd with heavens unbounded gains / Buryed the 7th Febr.1660.

3.   INSCRIPTION, PHILIP HUSTWAIT, 1788, CHANCEL.

An inscription plate which reads:

Beneath · this stone are deposited the remains of / Philip Hustwait a native of Bythorne, / who, in the 66th year of his age, / departed this transitory life, Feb.   12th 1788, / at Tempsford in the county of Bedford, / in hope, through the divine mercy, of a resurrection / to life & felicity eternal. / We know that if our earthly house of this tabernacle / were dissolved, we have a building of God, an house / not made with hands, eternal in the heavens.II Cor.V.1.

4.   INSCRIPTION, ELIZABETH RUGBY, n.d., LOST.

The Astry Manuscript notes a brass plate on the Chancel floor which read:

Here under buried rests Elizabeth / the loving faithfull & most vertuous wife / of Wm. Rugby whilst she drew her breath / 36 yeares with him she led her life / ptaking greefs & joys without all strife / 9 children she did beare him

9

nursed 8 / 5 still are living, 4 in moulds doe waite / with
her the joyful coming of ye Lord / who will judge all
according to his word.

COLNE

1. INDENT OF MILITARY, CANOPY, TWO SHIELDS, FOOT INSCRIPTION,
c1420, SOUTH AISLE.

This slab is said to have been re-fixed in a position corresponding
to its position in the old church. It shows a figure in plate
armour with a pointed bascinet, cross-hilted sword and misericorde
(small dagger). The feet rest against a lion. The figure is
surrounded by a canopy with side shafts, pinnacles and a trefoil
head. There were two shields in the canopy. In the 1880's the
slab was in the middle of the ruined chancel of the old church.

2. INDENT OF INSCRIPTION, SOUTH AISLE.

Also re-fixed in a position said to correspond to that in the old
church.

CONINGTON

1. INSCRIPTION, HENRY WILLIAMSON, 1613, MURAL, CHANCEL.

Clements noted the brass on the floor on the south side of the
Chancel, but it was lost for a period. It was ploughed up in the
fen in 1900, returned to the church in 1919 and screwed to the
wall. The brass, from the Southwark workshop, reads:

HIC JACET HENRICUS WILLIAMSON HUIUS ECCLE RECTOR, / SACRAE
THEOLOGIAE BACCALAUREUS ET CLARUS DIVINI VERBI / PRECO
DORMITORIU' HOC SIBI MORIENS ELEGIT. QUIESCAT / (INQUIT)
CORP' MEU' IN CUBILI ILLO IDQZ IN BEATA' RESURRECTIONEM /
ANIMA VERO MEA SUSCIPIAT DOM' JESUS VENI DOME JESU / VENI
CITO ET SUSCIPE ANIMA MEA SIC QUIEVIT IN DOMINO, / MARCII
VICESIMO SECUNDO DIE, ANO DNI 1613 / ROSA / DICTA HENRICI
RELICTA HAEC VERBA / LITERIS MEMORALIBUS INSCRIBI FECIT.

The word Rosa has the beginnings of the letter E engraved, which
suggests the name might have been Rosae.

Henry Williamson was instituted as Rector in 1603.

2. INDENT WITH CRUCIFIXION, MILITARY AND WIFE, BOTH KNEELING,
DOUBLE CANOPY, SHIELD, SCROLLS, MARGINAL INSCRIPTION, c1480,
NOW IN TOWER.

This curious brass on a shortened slab shows a crucifix in the
middle of the centre shaft of a double canopy. Two figures, both
with prayer scrolls, kneel on either side. The best illustration

of this indent is from a British Museum manuscript by J.Carter drawn in 1798 and reproduced in the VCH. The slab has been further shortened since Carter made his drawing and shows no traces of a marginal inscription or the bottom part of the kneeling figure. The slab also shows no traces of rivets; the indents are particularly shallow and the prayer scrolls unusually narrow.

COVINGTON

1. PORTION OF LOMBARDIC MARGINAL INSCRIPTION, CHANCEL.

A coffin shaped slab by the altar attributed to Richard de Bayeaux by a British Library manuscript. Only a few illegible letters are now visible. The Bayeux family were patrons of the living.

DIDDINGTON

1. WILLIAM TAYLARD, IN ARMOUR, UPPER HALF LOST AND WIFE, ELIZABETH, CANOPY, SCROLLS; PART OF CANOPY, CHILDREN, TWO SHIELDS AND TRINITY LOST, 1505, A.T.; SOUTH CHAPEL (M.S.I).

One of the most interesting brasses in the county, the upper part of the figure of William Taylard is lost, but known from a drawing in the Camden Visitation. This shows an heraldic tabard bearing:

1 & 4 **Taylard**: Quarterly argent and sable, a cross flory countercharged

2 & 3 **Chapell of Gamlingey**: Per fess azure and vert, a church with a steeple gules, between four escallops countercharged.

The colour given by Camden as azure should probably have been argent.

The lower part of the figure was loose in the 1880's and kept in the vicarage. Astry notes the presence of a shield over William's head bearing the arms of **Taylard**.

His wife wears an heraldic mantle and a pedimental head-dress. The mantle bears:

1. **Anstye:** Or, a cross engrailed, between four martlets gules

2. **Streete:** Vert, a fess between three horses courant argent

3. **Raynes:** Chequy, or and gules, a canton ermine

4. **Scudamore:** Gules, three stirrups or, leathered and buckled argent

Two scrolls remain:
1. **Fiat mia tua dne super nos**

11

2. Quaemodu sp'auim 'in te

Beneath the two figures is an inscription reading:

Wilellm Taylard piter cu conjuge grata / Elizabetha sibi nupta diu hac latitat urna / Mors vivos sepat separe cadaua nescit / Cu xpo vuiant hec viuet et ille quiescit / Anno Milesimo quigentesimo qqz quito / Vita privatur ppetua luce fruatur

On either side of the two figures are columns bearing saints. Those behind William Taylard are Salvator Mundi with his right hand raised bearing a globe and cross; St John the Baptist with a scroll and Agnus Dei (Holy Lamb); St John the Evangelist with chalice and serpent.

Behind his wife are the Virgin Mary with crown, sceptre and child; St Mary Magdalene with a box of ointment and St Catherine with a sword and wheel. St John the Evangelist holds the chalice with a serpent in it as a reminder of a challenge to him by the High Priest of the goddess Diana at Ephesus to drink a poisoned cup. St Mary Magdalene has the box of ointment with which she is said to have anointed Christ's body at the tomb. St Catherine was persecuted for her Christianity and tortured by being broken on a wheel.

Lost from the brass are the upper part of the canopy, five sons, seven daughters, a Trinity and two shields. One of the shields is known from a reference in the Astry Manuscript - that over the man - which bore the arms of Taylard.

William Taylard was Commissioner of Array in 1484 and a J.P. from 1461 until his death. His will requests burial at Diddington in the chapel of St Catherine on the north side of the church

2. ALICE TAYLARD, THREE SONS, BLESSED VIRGIN MARY, SHIELD, TWO OTHER PLATES, 1513, NAVE, (M.S.II).

The slab containing this brass was loose in the chancel in the last century, but is now set in the nave floor. It shows a woman in widow's dress - a kirtle, mantle, wimple and veil. From her mouth is a scroll bearing:

Jhu mcy lady help

Three sons kneel on a separate plate and above is an image of the Blessed Virgin Mary, crowned, seated and holding a child. The shield bears:

Taylard impaling Forster: Sable, a chevron ermine between three pheons or.

On either side of the shield is a small plate each bearing the date 1513, the dexter between three fleur-de-lys; the sinister between three pheons. The inscription is now lost.

In her will, proved March 30, 1513, she asks to be buried at Diddington and that "all my landes and ten'tes in London be in guyding of my brother Mr Wm.Taylard, doctor, for 16 yeares, to the entent he shall bring up my two children,. Lawrence and Giles...."

EATON SOCON

1. JOHN COVESGROVE IN CIVIL DRESS AND WIFE, TWO SCROLLS MUTILATED, MARGINAL INSCRIPTION LOST, c1400, MURAL, CHANCEL, (M.S.I).

Formerly on a slab at the east end of the North Aisle, the remains of this brass are fixed to the wall of the Nave. Before the church was gutted by fire in 1930 there were also indents of a marginal inscription with evangelical symbols at the corners. The male figure shows a civilian in a long gown with close fitting sleeves. This is buttoned at the front with a hood folded back round the neck. His wife is dressed in a longer gown with a veil head-dress. With the figures are the remains of two mouth scrolls parts of which have disappeared since Gough recorded them.

That from the man reads (bracketed portions remaining) :

Qui (venturus es judica)re vivos & mortuos

From the woman :

Tunc (d'ne dona nobis requiem sempiternam)

Part of the woman's scroll has been incorrectly attached to the other scroll.

The inscription in Gough's time read:

Hic jacent Johannes Covesgrove de Eton qui obiit xiii die mensis Septembr...

Much the same remained c1800 although it had been largely lost by 1846 and completely gone by about 1890. Two of the evangelical symbols remained when Gough saw the brass - St John and St Matthew. The illustration comes from Fisher who must have drawn it at much the same period as Gough's visit.

2. LADY; HUSBAND AND INSCRIPTION LOST, c1450, NOW IN LOCKED CASE, (M.S.II).
This Series B brass was formerly in the Nave, but following the fire in which it was severely damaged, the figure was lifted and

13

placed in a glass case with other relics. A poor rubbing in the Cambridge Collection shows the already worn figure of a woman in a loose sleeved gown and veil head-dress. On the slab, which is now lost, were the indents of a civilian and a foot inscription, below which was the indent of a quadrangular plate. The plate may have been a later addition bearing an inscription to another person.

3.   INSCRIPTION, ELENA WAWTON, 1458, MURAL IN NAVE, (M.S.III).

Now fixed to one of the tower piers, this inscription was loose in the church chest c1846. Before the fire it was fixed to a board. It reads:

Hic jacet d'na Elena Wawton quondam / uxoris d'ni Thome Wawton militis que / obiit v die mense ffebruarii A d'ni mil'mo / CCCCLVIII cui' anime p'picietur deus Ame.

4.   TWO SONS; CIVILIAN AND WIFE, DAUGHTERS, SHIELD AND INSCRIPTION LOST, c1570, CHANCEL, (M.S.IV).

Now partially covered by a fixed carpet, the only portion remaining is a small plate showing two boys in long gowns with false sleeves and a scarf attached to the waist. The indent of their father shows him in a short cloak probably standing on a tiled floor. Under the carpet is the indent of a woman and beneath her a small plate, probably engraved with her daughters. Above the figures is the indent of a shield which, as it was made of lead, was probably lost in the fire. A rubbing in the Cambridge Collection shows:

Wawton (or Walton): Argent, a chevron gules between three bugle horns gules, stringed or, a crescent for difference impaling Conquest: Quarterly argent and sable, overall a label of three points (countercharged?).

5.   INSCRIPTION, ELIZABETH BRACKIN, 1655, NOW LOST, (M.S.V).

Formerly on the Nave floor, by 1930 it was on a board in the Nave and then lost in the fire. It read:

HERE UNDER LYETH INTERR'D THE BODY OF / MRS ELIZABETH BRACKIN LATE WIFE TO JOHN / BRACKIN OF EATON SOCON IN THE COUNTY OF / BEDFORD ESQ WHO DEPARTED THIS LIFE / THE 28TH OF NOVEMBER ANNO DNI:1655 / BEFORE WHOM WAS IN THIS PLACE BURIED / MRS ELIZABETH BRACKIN THEIR DAUGHTER / WHO DYED THE 28TH OF DECEMBER / ANNOQZ DNI: 1650

6.   INSCRIPTION AND ARMS, J.BEVERLEY, 1661, NOW LOST.

This was present c1800 and consisted of a brass shield and inscription cut into the stone. The shield bore:
Beverley: Argent, a fess dancetty sable between three leopard's faces or.

7.   LOMBARDIC MARGINAL INSCRIPTION,   NOW LOST.

Gough   noted a blue coffin shaped slab in the South Aisle which   by 1890 had been moved to the Nave.   The only decipherable portion was :

LAM : LE or DE : B....:

8.   INDENT OF CIVILIAN, WIFE, FOOT INSCRIPTION,   ABOUT EIGHT CHILDREN, TWO SMALL CIRCULAR INDENTS AT BASE, NOW LOST.

Formerly in the Chancel on the North side.

9.   INDENT OF CIVILIAN, WIFE, FOOT INSCRIPTION, c1480,   NOW LOST.

Formerly in the Nave.

10.   INDENT OF CIVILIAN, WIFE, FOOT INSCRIPTION, NOW LOST.

Two half figures, described as a good brass of the late 14th or early 15th Century, in the Nave.

11.   INDENT OF LARGE SHIELD, NOW LOST.

This was formerly on the Chancel floor and was probably the indent of No.6.

12.   INDENT OF LARGE QUADRANGULAR PLATE, NAVE.

Probably the indent of No.5.

13.   INDENTS.

Gough c1790 and the Topographer and Genealogist,   c1846 noted "several brassless monuments of priests and others".

N.B.   Two of the lost indents may be on the tower floor underneath furniture.

ELTON

1.   INDENT OF CIVILIAN, WIFE, ONE SON, ABOUT FOUR DAUGHTERS, RELIGIOUS SYMBOL, SHIELD, FOOT INSCRIPTION, SOUTH PORCH.

This was removed from the church at some period.

2.   INDENT OF ECCLESIASTIC, FOOT INSCRIPTION, NOW LOST.

Gough's manuscript in the Bodleian notes this as being in the Nave.

3. INDENT OF MAN, WOMAN, ONE SHIELD ABOVE HIM, THREE BY HER, A SQUARE ABOVE THEM AND A SHIELD.

Gough lists this in the South Aisle and it is almost certainly the indent now in the South Porch.

4. INDENT.

Gough notes "in the South Porch is the matrix of a brass". This is probably the surviving indent.

5. MILITARY FIGURE IN TABARD, KNEELING.

The Camden Visitation shows the drawing of a military figure, the tabard bearing the arms: ? Argent, a chevron gules between three eagles(?) displayed.

This is probably a figure from a stained glass window, now lost.

EVERTON

1. INDENT OF ECCLESIASTIC, c1450, NAVE.

Indent showing an ecclesiastic in mass vestments

2. INDENT OF MILITARY, WIFE, MARGINAL INSCRIPTION, EVANGELICAL SYMBOLS, FOUR SHIELDS, ONE SON, ONE DAUGHTER, c1500, NAVE.

The slab has cracked in the middle, the two parts being re-joined in 1903.

EYNESBURY

1. INDENT OF CIVILIAN, WIFE AND INSCRIPTION, c1480, SOUTH AISLE.

On a worn slab at the west end of the South Aisle are the indents of two small figures from the Cambridge workshop.

2. INDENT OF CIVILIAN, THREE WIVES, FOOT INSCRIPTION, c1500, SOUTH AISLE.

The slab, the two parts of which were separated prior to 1900 was rejoined when the paving fell into a vault, and shows the indents of Cambridge workshop brasses. The ladies wear a distinctive cap.

3. RIVETS, TRACES OF MARGINAL INSCRIPTION AND EVANGELICAL SYMBOLS, c1580, NORTH PORCH.

This extremely worn slab showed, according to Macklin, a lady in a Paris hat kneeling at a prayer desk, with an inscription below.

4. INDENT OF CANOPY, TWO SHIELDS, MARGINAL INSCRIPTION .

The RCHM records a fragment of a slab in the Rectory Garden with the remains of an indent, probably late 14th - early 15th Century. A drawing in the Norris Library and Museum shows at least a double canopy, which suggests there would have been at least two figures.

5. LOMBARDIC MARGINAL INSCRIPTION, NOW LOST.

Gorham records, in the middle of the South Aisle, a grey marble slab with a Lombardic marginal inscription which read:

RICHARD : DE : ... : GIST : ICI : ... DE : SA : ALME : VRA : MERCI

6. BRASS TO VALENTINE FYNCHE, NOW LOST.

Gorham notes a fragment of brass, not more ancient than early in the reign of Elizabeth, with the name **Valentine Fynche**. Fynche was living in 15 Edward VI as appears from the baptism of a child.

FENSTANTON

1. INDENT OF DEMI-ECCLESIASTIC, LOMBARDIC MARGINAL INSCRIPTION, c1350, CHANCEL.

This large Purbeck marble slab in the middle of the Chancel has the indent of the bust of a priest with a strip of brass above the head The marginal inscription, which may not have been brass inlay, reads:

HIC : JACET : DOMINUS : WILELMUS : DE : LOUGTHONE (or LONGTHORNE) : QUONDAM : RECTOR : HUIUS : ECCLESIE : ET : FUNDATOR : HUIUS : CA(PELL)E or CA(NTARI)E.

It may possibly commemorate William de Loughton, Rector 1345-52.

GLATTON

1. INSCRIPTION, CATHERINE SHERRARD, 1724, MURAL, SOUTH AISLE.

The polished copper plate in a wooden frame reads:

Catherine Sherrard / Aged 63 years / Died December the 16th / 1724

GODMANCHESTER

1. CIVILIAN; TWO WIVES, CHILDREN AND FOOT INSCRIPTION LOST, c1520, MURAL, NORTH AISLE.

Formerly on a slab in the Nave, now hidden under a raised platform, which shows the indents of two wives in pedimental head-dresses, two groups of children and a foot inscription. The figure shows a man in a fur-lined gown, a belt and gypciere. A Bodleian manuscript says that c1800 one of the wives and twelve sons remained. A photograph of a poor rubbing in the Norris Library and Museum shows the bottom of the figure apparently complete.

The brass was removed when the flooring was laid and probably damaged then or shortly afterwards as a small piece had been broken off the bottom by 1981. The brass was taken to the Egan workshop in Milton Keynes for repair and setting into wood. It was returned in 1983 and fixed to the wall. The brass had been loose previously as there was evidence of a (bodged) refixing, probably in the 19th Century.

2.   INDENT OF INSCRIPTION, CHANCEL.

This is recorded by the RCHM, but is now covered. There is a measured drawing of it in the Norris Library and Museum.

GREAT GRANSDEN

1.   INDENT OF CROSS FLORY WITH DEMI-ECCLESIASTIC IN HEAD, LOMBARDIC MARGINAL INSCRIPTION, THOMAS DE NEUSOM, c1330, MURAL, TOWER. (No. 1 on plan)

This huge slab was formerly in the middle of the Chancel as shown by an 1834 drawing by Le Grice in the Huntingdonshire Record Office. At the 1873 restoration it was moved to the churchyard at the east end of the Chancel. A few years later it was brought back into the church, the surface polished, the letters badly re-cut and the slab set up against the North wall of the tower. The stem of the cross rises from a lion and the figure shows a priest in eucharist vestments. The inscription to this former rector who was instituted in 1301 and died c1327 reads:

   HIC : JACET : THOMAS : DE : NEUSAM : QUONDAM : RECTOR :
   ISTIUS : ECCLESIE : CUIUS : ANIME : PROPICIETUR : DEUS

2.   INDENT OF DEMI-ECCLESIASTIC ABOVE A PLAIN CROSS, MARGINAL INSCRIPTION WITH EVANGELICAL SYMBOLS AT CORNERS, c1425, NOW LOST. (No. 2 on plan)

In 1748 the Rev.Wm.Cole saw this at the east end of the South Aisle, a position confirmed by Le Grice. At the restoration it was moved into the churchyard and is now buried near the South Porch.

3.   INDENT OF ECCLESIASTIC ABOVE CROSS, SCROLL AND FOOT INSCRIPTION, c1430, NOW LOST. (No. 3 on plan)

Cole noted this in the Nave, which is confirmed by a pre-1873 photograph in the Huntingdonshire Record Office. The priest wore a cassock, surplice and almuce; the cross rises from steps and is rounded at the intersection of the arms. It is buried now in the churchyard at the east end of the Chancel.

4. INDENT OF CIVILIAN, WIFE, FOOT INSCRIPTION, ANOTHER LADY BELOW, c1480, NOW LOST. (No. 4 on plan)

Cole noted this in the Chancel at the head of the Neusom indent, but Le Grice shows it at the side. It is now buried in the churchyard near No.2.

N.B. Le Grice states that all the brass had gone before 1832.

GREAT STAUGHTON

1. INDENT OF TWO FIGURES, SCROLLS, TWO INSCRIPTION PLATES, TWO GROUPS OF CHILDREN, SHROUD ABOVE FIGURES, FOUR EMBLEMS, CHANCEL.

Now covered by a fixed carpet, the indent is unusual as it includes the indent of a figure in a shroud above the two main effigies of a man and wife.

2. INDENT OF SHIELD, CHANCEL

The remainder of the slab is covered and almost certainly contains more. Possibly the slab for No.5. A letter in the Norris Library and Museum says that when the organ was moved in 1889, the indents of two more shields were found on the slab.

3. INDENT OF TWO SHIELDS, INSCRIPTION, CHANCEL.

The two shields are across the upper part of the slab and the inscription plate across the middle.

4. RIVETS.

The RCHM records a worn indent with rivets in the Chancel, probably now covered by a fixed carpet.

5. DRAWING OF MILITARY FIGURE IN TABARD, WIFE IN MANTLE, FOUR SHIELDS, NOW LOST.

The 1613 Visitation has the drawing of a military figure in plate armour with a tabard bearing: Wauton: Argent, a chevron, in dexter chief an annulet. On her mantle the wife bears: ? : on a chevron three crosses pattee.

The Wauton family held the Manor of Great Staughton and the brass may commemorate Thomas Wauton who died in 1436 or his son, also called Thomas, date of death unknown.

6. INSCRIPTION, JOHN GAUL, 1687, NOW LOST.

Clements records a brass plate on the Chancel floor which read:

> Memoriae Sacrum / Hic jacet venerabilis admordum Rexex
> Magister Johannes Gaule Theologus consummatus / et omnibus
> numeris absolutus; scriptor Nervossus / et acutus:
> consianatur Egregius et assiduus Constans / ubique Ecclesie
> et Majestatiis Reginae Assentor (nec Florentis magis /
> utruisque quam afflictae) Idemq: Perduellium et schismaticae
> / Factionis propugnator acerrimus : Qui cum deo et Muneri
> suo / in Evangelio per annos quinquagenta sex (et quod
> excurrit) / Summa cum Fide et Diligentia in hac Parochia
> Duserrisset / Octogesimum Sextum Aetatis suae annum Agens ad
> Coelum / aspiravit Anima VIII die Mensis Julii Anno Salutis
> MDCLXXXVII.

7. INSCRIPTION, ROBERT STONHAM, 1464, NOW LOST.

An inscription is given in the Visitation, but it may not be
brass.

N.B. The Edwardian Inventory's list of church goods sold or
stolen at Gt Staughton includes "vii stonn of latten and brasse".
Some of this could have been memorial brass.

GREAT STUKELEY

1. INDENT OF MILITARY FIGURE SUPERIMPOSED ON CROSS, TWO FIGURES, TWO CHILDREN, SHIELD, MARGINAL INSCRIPTION, EVANGELICAL SYMBOLS, NORTH AISLE.

This interesting indent originally consisted of a cross, c1410
rising from a mount. The figures at either side and the two
children beneath were added later, but certainly not as late as
the military figure which was added c1460. This was the brass to
Sir Nicholas Styvele and two drawings of it exist, both by the
Antiquarian William Stukeley. This also shows a shield which bears
Stukeley: Argent, on a fess, sable three mullets of the field.

Prior to 1759 the brass was fixed on a wall in the Hall, but then
refixed in the church. The marginal inscription was loose at that
time in the parish chest. The figure was moved again in 1764 and
placed in a mausoleum in Kentish Town. All trace has now been
lost. The indent was covered by tiles c1850 and uncovered in 1910
when it was moved and re-set in the same position.

2. INDENT OF MILITARY, FOOT INSCRIPTION, c1470, NAVE.

The indent is filled partially with cement and a note in the Cambridge Collection says the slab was used for mixing mortar and
cement at a restoration.

3. INSCRIPTION, WILLIAM STEWKELE, NOW LOST.

The Astry manuscript notes, in the North Aisle of the church, a brass border on a blue marble stone with these words remaining:

.....the soule of William Stewkeley ...to God... on whose soule Jesu ...

HAMMERTON

1. INSCRIPTION, RICHARD NEWMAN, 1663, NOW LOST.

The only record of this brass is in the Astry manuscript which reads: "in ye chancell o' th' ground is this following inscription in brass :

Richardus Newman, S.T.B., Rector huius Ecclesie annos 29 natus 1 die Jan. 1590. Denatus 19 Junii 1663. Hic in pace quiescit."

HARTFORD

1. BRASS TO ROBERT CROSS, NOW LOST.

Clements notes a brass fixed to the Chancel wall inscribed:

Positae exuvide Robti Cross

HELPSTONE

1. INDENT OF CROSS, BUST OF PRIEST IN HEAD, TWO SHIELDS, LOMBARDIC MARGINAL INSCRIPTION, ROGER DE HEGHAM, 1320, NORTH AISLE.

This particularly fine brass has been progressively covered over the years - the last portion to disappear being in August 1983 a week or so before the photograph was taken. Earlier descriptions from a variety of sources note this as the indent of a foliated quartrefoil cross containing the bust of a priest / in an amice supported by a slender stem with three pairs of leaves radiating from it at intervals and a lion passant at the foot. There are two small shields on either side of the cross. The marginal inscription reads:

ICI : GIST : ROGER : DE : HEGHAM : DE : KY : DEU : DOYNT : REPOS : E : KY : PUR : SA : ALME : PRIERA : III : CCC : JOURS : DE : PARDOUN : AVERA

2. INDENT OF LOMBARDIC MARGINAL INSCRIPTION, NOW LOST.

Noted by Bridges.

3. INDENT OF PRIEST, NAVE, NOW LOST.

21

Noted by Paley. The VCH for Northants. records an indent in the middle aisle for a single figure and a marginal inscription.

HEMINGFORD ABBOTS

1. INDENT OF CROSS, LOMBARDIC MARGINAL INSCRIPTION, CHANCEL.

Partly hidden by modern seating, the stem of a cross runs up the centre of the slab, with a marginal inscription reading:

...(PERSU)NE : DE : LE : EGLISE : DE : (H)EMYN(GF)ORD....

HEMINGFORD GREY

1. INDENT OF ECCLESIASTIC, FOOT INSCRIPTION, NOW LOST.

When the Rev. Cole visited in 1744 he noted an old grey marble in the middle of the Nave which had the indent of a small figure of a priest and a foot inscription beneath it.

HILTON

1. INDENT OF CIVILIAN, FOOT INSCRIPTION, c1540, NAVE.

In the middle of the Nave is a slab with the worn indent of a figure and a foot inscription. The indent is described either as a priest or civilian in a long gown. Probably a civilian although it is too worn to be certain.

2. FIGURE, INSCRIPTION, ROGER CROWNTOFT, 1529, NOW LOST.

Clements records in the middle aisle the picture of a man in brass in the habit "of those times" and this inscription:

Here lieth Roger Crowntoft, sumtyme marchaunt of ye Staple whiche dep'd to God the xii day of M'che the yre of or Lorde MCCCCCXXIX on whose soule and all cristen solls Jesu have mercy.

Almost certainly the brass belonging to indent 1.

HUNTINGDON, ALL SAINTS

1. INSCRIPTION, RICHARD LEVET, 1506, NOW LOST.

In 1824 Carruthers described this as being on a narrow strip of brass in a dark blue marble slab on the floor near the pulpit. It is now lost, but probably survived until about 1890. There is a rubbing of it in the Cambridge Collection. An undated manuscript at the Norris Library and Museum, St Ives says this was on a gravestone in the middle of the church and there seems to have been a figure.   The inscription read:

Hic   jacet Ricus Levet alias Oyler de Wysbyche q' obiit   xxvi
die ffebruary,   A dni MCCCCCVI cui aie ppiciet de.

2.   INSCRIPTION, ROBERT NEWELL,   1509,   NOW LOST.

An inscription inscription,   from sewhich read:es read:

Orate pro animab' Roberti   Newell quondam Burgensis de
Huntingdon   et Agnetis consortis suae qui quidem Robtus obiit
xx die mensis Februarii A Dni 1509 cujus animabus etc.

3.   INSCRIPTION, ROGER HEYNS,   1518,   NOW LOST.

From the same sources,   the inscription read:

Hic   jacet Rogerus Heyns quondam Burgensis villae Huntingdon
et Elena uxor ejus qui quidem Rogerus obiit 25 die mens
Januarii An Dni 1518 quorum aiabs propiciet Deus.

4.   INSCRIPTION, THOMAS BEARD,   1631,   NOW LOST.

Probably at the entrance to the Chancel, this inscription from the
Astry manuscript read:

Ego Thomas Beard Sacre Theologie Professor in Ecclesia omnium
Sanctorum Huntingdoniae Verbi Divini Praedicator olim.   Jam
sanus sum.   Obiit Januarii 8 An.   1631.

Thomas   Beard   was Master of the Free Grammar School at   Huntingdon
and   had   Oliver   Cromwell as one of his pupils.   He was   a   major
influence   on   the young Cromwell at an impressionable   age.   The
Puritan   Doctor Beard is described by Antonia Fraser as a   striking
example   of   the   sort   of   men,   intellectual,   proselytizing,
courageous,   above   all   determined to   sort out honestly the
relationship   of   God to man and the correct part to be played in
this   by   the   church,   who made up the body of the   early English
Puritans.   He   was   Rector of All Saints from 1601 and   a   former
Rector of Wistow and St John Baptist,   Huntingdon.

5.   BRASS OF MILITARY, WIFE, SHIELDS, NOW LOST.

Carruthers and Brayley describe a very large blue slab close to the
pulpit   bearing   the   figures of a knight and his wife   with   their
armorial   bearings.   It is suggested by Macklin that this was   the
brass   to   Sir Henry Cromwell,   the main builder of   Hinchingbrooke
House,   who   was known as the Golden Knight because of his   lavish
hospitality.

6.   INDENTS.

Carruthers and Brayley, one probably copying the other, note several gravestones in the Nave, one or two in the West Transverse Aisle and other parts of the church which displayed indents.

N.B. A note in the Norris Library and Museum states that slabs containing indents were broken up for concrete when Sir Gilbert Scott restored the church in 1859.

HUNTINGDON ST MARY'S

1. INDENT OF TWO QUARTREFOILS, SOUTH AISLE.

On the portion of the slab used now as a step from the Aisle to the South Porch are the indents of two quartrefoils, probably evangelical symbols, once forming part of a larger brass.

2. OTHER INDENTS.

Carruthers noted that in the North Aisle was a dark grey marble slab bearing the indents of brasses which formed an ogee arch with rich ornamented tracery on either side. In the South Aisle there were also marks of brasses, all now lost.

KEYSTON

1. INDENT OF CIVILIAN, WIFE, DEVICES, NORTH TRANSEPT.

On the west wall in a slab of local stone are the deep cut indents of man and his wife, with inscription plate below. There is a device and a letter D on the right hand side and a monogram on the other, probably not contemporary. This early 16th Century slab has been re-set.

LEIGHTON BROMSWOLD

1. INDENT OF ECCLESIASTIC, FOOT INSCRIPTION, TOWER FLOOR.

Against the Tower door, almost certainly not in its original position.

LITTLE GIDDING

1. INSCRIPTION AND SHIELD, MARY MAPLETOFT, 1656, MURAL, NAVE, (M.S.I).

On a rectangular plate, the arms are within a Jacobean frame with grotesque faces on the scrolls. The arms are: **Mapletoft**: Argent, on on a chevron between three cross-crosslets or, on a chief argent, a lion passant gules impaling **Collet**: Sable, on a chevron between three hinds trippant argent, as many annulets of the first. The inscription reads:

HERE LYETH YE BODY OF MARY / MAPLETOFT ELDEST DAUGHTER OF SOL / OMON MAPLETOFT & JUDETH HIS WIFE & / GRANDCHILD TO JOHN AND SUSANNA COLLET.   SHE DIED YE 14 OF JULY 1656

The Astry manuscript notes this as being on a raised stone.

2.   INSCRIPTION, ACHIEVEMENT, JOHN FARRAR, 1657, MURAL, NAVE, (M.S.II).

This is a palimpsest brass, the reverse bearing an inscription from Psalm 37, Verse 27. It is probably one of the texts hung up in the community of Little Gidding and subsequently re-used as a memorial. The reverse reads:

FLEE FROM EVILL / AND / DOE YE THINGE YT IS GOOD / AND / DWELL FOR EVERMORE

On the obverse side the arms are: **Ferrar:** on a bend cotised sable, three horseshoes of the first. Crest: Or, on an esquire's helmet with a bold scrolled mantle gules, doubled argent, on a wreath or and sable an arm embowed in scaled armour proper, the hand grasping grasping a broken sword argent, hilt and pommel or. The inscription reads:

HERE LIETH THE BODY OF / JOHN FARRAR ESQR LORD OF / THIS MANNOUR WHO DEPARTED / THIS LIFE YE 28TH OF SEPTbr 1657

A note in the Huntingdonshire Record Office records the brass on a raised stone in the churchyard - Dugdale also saw it there in 1815.

3.   INSCRIPTION, SUSANNA COLLET, 1657, MURAL, NAVE, (M.S.III).

The Astry manuscript suggests this was on the same stone as No.10. The inscription reads:

HERE ALSO SLEEPETH SUSANA / WIFE TO JOHN COLLET, ESOR. / BY WHOM SHE HAD ISSUE 8 SONNS / & 8 DAUGHTERS. SHE WAS YE ONLY / DAUGHTER OF MR NICHOLAS FARRAR / OF LONDON MERCHANT & SISTER TO / JOHN FARRER ESQR LATE LD OF THIS MANOR / WHO DIED YE 9th OCTbr 1657 AGED 76 YEARS.

4.   INSCRIPTION ANN FERRAR, 1702, MURAL, NAVE, (M.S.IV).

A small rectangular brass bearing this inscription:

Here lyeth the Body of / Ann ye Wife of John Ferrar / Esq. who departed this life / the 8th of March 1702 / She was the daughter of / Sr Tho.   Brook

5.   INSCRIPTION AND ARMS, ELEANOR GODDARD, 1717, MURAL, NAVE, (M.S.V).

A large square plate with the arms between two banners both bearing emblems of mortality. The arms on the lozenge are: **Goddard**: Gules, a chevron vair, between three crescents argent impaling **Long**: a a chevron between three lions rampant. The inscription reads:

> Here sleepeth Eleanor Goddard / Daughter to George Long of /
> London Merchant & Relict / of James Goddard of Marston / in
> Wilts. Gent. who died April / the 20th 1717.

6. INSCRIPTION AND ACHIEVEMENT, JOHN FERRAR, 1719, MURAL, NAVE, (M.S.VI).

The achievement bears: **Ferrar** impaling **Brooke**: Or, a cross engrailed quarterly gules and sable. The inscription reads:

> HERE LYETH THE BODY OF / JOHN FERRAR ESQ LORD / OF THIS
> MANNOUR WHO / DEPARTED THIS LIFE FEBR / THE 23 1719 AGED 89.

7. FOUR INDENTS OF INSCRIPTIONS IN CHURCHYARD.

In the path leading to the door of the church are four indents for brasses 2, 3, 4 and 5.

8. CREED BEHIND ALTAR.

Although not a memorial brass, this appears to have come from the same source. It was bought by Mary Ferrar, the mother of Nicholas Ferrar, who died in 1634.

9. INSCRIPTION AND ARMS, MARGARET LEGAT, 1648, NOW LOST.

A manuscript in the University Library, Cambridge notes this as engraved in brass on a stone. The arms were: **Legat**(?): Ermine, a lion rampant impaling **Collet**. The inscription read:

> Here lyeth the body of Margaret Legat, daughter of Thomas
> Posthumus Legat of Essex Esqr. & Margaret his wife and
> grandchild to John and Susanna Collet. She died an infant
> on the 17th day of September 1648.

10. INSCRIPTION AND ARMS, JOHN COLLET, 1650, NOW LOST.

The Astry manuscript records this on a brass plate on a raised stone with the arms of **Collet** impaling **Ferrar**. The crest: a hind. The inscription read:

> Here lyeth ye body of John Collet esq. aged 79 yeares who
> died ye 29 of March 1650.

11. INSCRIPTION AND ARMS, SUSANNA CHEDLEY, 1657, NOW LOST.

Also from Astry who noted it on a stone near the ground. The arms are described as "in brass these coats in pale (or ye wife between her two husbands)" and were: **Mapletoft, Collet, Legat.** The inscription read:

> The remains of Susanna Chedley first to Josuah Mapletoft wife, afterwards to James Chedley, daughter to John and Susanna Collet who exchanged their life for a better on ye 31st day of October in ye year of our Lord 1657 & of her pilgrimage fifty and five. Viram bonam Mors aux bona exrivit aut nulla.

N.B. In establishing the link between these brasses, this abbreviated pedigree may be useful:

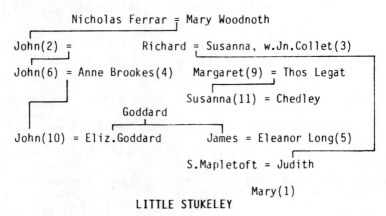

Nicholas Ferrar = Mary Woodnoth

John(2) =   Richard = Susanna, w.Jn.Collet(3)

John(6) = Anne Brookes(4)   Margaret(9) = Thos Legat

Susanna(11) = Chedley

Goddard

John(10) = Eliz.Goddard   James = Eleanor Long(5)

S.Mapletoft = Judith

Mary(1)

LITTLE STUKELEY

1. ECCLESIASTIC, c 1620, SOUTH AISLE, (M.S.I).

Re-set in 1887, the brass shows an ecclesiastic in a long gown with false hanging sleeves covering doublet and hose. On his head is a skull cap. This is the brass to William Halles who died in 1618. An inscription in Clements notes:

> Quam tegit hic tumulus quaris tegit Olegit illium / Cui vix invenit secula nostra parem / Quam tegit ille Pater, fuit hic Pastorque fidelis / Steuclia pastorem--- patrem / sanc Pater Pastore fuit praestantior ipse / Nesscio : sed Pater et pastor amandus erat / Dum Pastor passcebat ores, passecebat orrelas / exmplo Verbo, demique pane suo / Dum Pater en quanqun numerosa prole beatus / Ut semper sum istis sit bene cura fuit / Ut Pater et pastor fruiter semperque fructur / Deliciis, Caelo, prosperitate, Deo / Gulielmus Halles obiit octavo Die Augusti / Anno Domini 1618.

The brass was probably loose before refixing. William Halles was instituted in 1581.

2. INDENT OF LOMBARDIC INSCRIPTION, POSSIBLY NOW LOST.

The Victoria County History records part of a 14th Century slab with an inscription in Lombardic letters:

....E LA NOKE GIS .....L'ALME E....

Possibly not brass, it may commemorate Richard de la Noke who held the manor in 1346.

LONG STOW (or STOW LONGA)

1. INSCRIPTION, SIR THOMAS MAPLES, 1634, ANOTHER PLATE LOST, MURAL, CHANCEL, (M.S.I).

This is one of two plates, the other being lost, on a freestone tablet with fluted side pilasters, entablature and cresting with shield of arms. The inscription reads:

HERE LIETH SR THOMAS MAPLES BARONETT / WAITINGE FOR THE IMMEDIATE COMEING / OF HIS Saviour Jesus / Obiit Feb: 13, 1634

2. INDENT OF CROSS, FOOT INSCRIPTION, 15TH CENTURY, CHANCEL.

On the Chancel floor is the indent of a fine floriated cross.

3. INSCRIPTION, AGNES MAPLES, 1624, NOW LOST.

This is almost certainly the missing plate from the monument to Sir Thomas Maples. The inscription is from a manuscript at the Cambridge University Library and read:

Here lyeth Agnes ye wife of Thomas Maples Esq. who / was buried ye 26 of August 1624 / All natures parts and graces all devine / In her excell'd, in her they all did shine / To Husband kynde, he her beyond all measure / Esteemed his jewell and his chiefest treasure / For whose sake onely, onely for her sake / For widdowes three, three houses he did make / Herself, her Christ with open arms receaved her / Hence death of life most cruelly bereaved her

4. INSCRIPTION, ROBERT DORRINGTON, 1615, NOW LOST.

The same source as the last gives this as being on a brass plate on the ground:

Here lieth buried Mr Robert Dorrington, Gent., who was of ye age of LXXII yeares and departed this life ye first of June Anno Dni 1615. Memoriae Sacrum. / We find all honour age, but vertue more / Yet age and virtue joined with God's great feare / Also God and all good men doe love, therefore / Finding also age, virtue and piety here / Then stay and reade, though grave hath lodged a guest / Time age ye world his name, yet God the rest. / Vertus laudatur et alget.

28

5.   INSCRIPTION, ELLYNOR DORRINGTON, 1616, NOW LOST.

From the same source as the last :

> An epitaph of ye death of Mrs Ellynor Dorrington late wife of
> Robert Dorrington of Stowe in ye county of Huntingdon, Gent.
> who was buried ye 28th day of Aprill Anno Dni 1616....
> about....years.   / Here lies God's love who while in life
> she was to her / children, neighbours, friends and kyn / A
> joy and stay and now a looking glasse for them to see / the
> state life standeth in / Then sith alive and dead she vertue
> gives / Her praises cannot dy while vertue lives.   / Vivit
> post fuera virtus.

LONGTHORPE

1.   INSCRIPTION, GEORGE LEAFIELD, 1685, NOW LOST.

Sweeting quotes a British Library manuscript (not traced) that in
1771 this inscription was on a brass plate measuring about a foot
square near the entrance to the Chancel:

> Cum refectum et Deo (coemeterii gratia) sacratum hoc fuit
> saellum Anno Dom 1683 hoc primum Auxilii autimanu posuit
> saxum Gulielmus filius natu maximus Georgii Leafield Armigeri
> sub quo eodem saxo a dedicatione ipse primus corpore tenui
> sepultus erat Decemb.   21 Anno Dom 1685 aetatis 8.

A footnote says the brass was too worn to be entirely read.

2.   INSCRIPTION, MATTHEW AND DOROTHY BOOTH, 1713, NOW LOST.

Sweeting also noted this brass beside No.1.   It was a very similar
one to the two children of Matthew Booth, writing master, and
Dorothy, his wife, dated 1709 and 1713.

MARHOLM

1.   SIR WILLIAM FITZWILLIAM, IN ARMOUR WITH TABARD, AND WIFE, ANNE, IN HERALDIC MANTLE, ELEVEN SHIELDS, INSCRIPTION, 1534, A.T., CHANCEL, (M.S.I).

The brass was repaired in 1674 when the upper part of the male
figure and two shields were renewed and an inscription and two more
shields added.   There were further minor changes in the heraldry
at another restoration in 1970.   The earlier restoration may have
been required as a result of damage during the Civil War when the
church is believed to have been set on fire.   The lower half of
the male figure is London work showing typical armour of the
period.   The upper part is Seventeenth Century work.   The wife
wears a long gown covered with an heraldic mantle and a pedimental
head-dress.   The centre plate, bearing the later inscription,

covers an indent, probably of a Trinity or other religious symbol. It reads:

> THESE MONUMENTS / WERE REPAIRED & BEAUTIFIED / BY YE RT HONBL WILLIAM / LORD FITZWILLIAM ANO 1674

The earlier inscription beneath the two figures reads:

> Syr Wylliam Fytzwyllyms Knyght Decessyd the ix / daye of August in the xxvi yere of or Soverayn lorde / kyng Henry the viii in Anno dni MCCCCCXXXIIII / and lyeth beuried under thys Tombe

There are two scrolls both reading: **Prohibere nephas.** This is from Virgil's Aeneid and may be translated as "Restrain us from wrong doing".

The heraldry is complex and reads:

TABARD

Fitzwilliams: Lozengy argent and gules

MANTLE - dexter side

1. **Fitzwilliams**

2. **Driby of Tattershall:** Argent, three cinquefoils gules, a canton of the last

3. **Warenne:** Chequy or and azure.

MANTLE - sinister side

Hawes: Azure, on a chevron or, three cinquefoils gules, on a canton argent, a lion passant gules quartering **Grene of York:** Or, fretty gules, a fess per fess dancetty point in point azure and ermine.

The shields on Sir William's side bear:

1. **Fitzwilliams** impaling **Solabis:** Argent, a fess gules between two bars nebulee sable. **N.B.** This shield is smaller than the others and may be of an earlier date.

2. **Fitzwilliams** impaling **Elmley:** Sable, a wildman or wreathed and girded vert, holding an uprooted tree stump proper.

3. **Fitzwilliams** and **Warenne** quarterly impaling **Lacy:** Or, a lion rampant purpure;

4. **Fitzwilliams** and **Warenne** quarterly impaling **Deyncourt:** Argent, a

a fess dancetty between ten billets of the second, four, two, three and one;

5. **Fitzwilliams** impaling ? : Chequy within a bordure. **N.B.** In the 1970 restoration this shield was painted over and now bears: Or, an orle sable.

The shields on the wife's side bear:

1. **Fitzwilliams** impaling **Warenne**

2. **Fitzwilliams** quartering **Warenne** impaling **Lacy** quartering **Lacy** (alternative coat): Quarterly or and gules, overall a bendlet with a label of five points argent

3. **Fitzwilliams**

4. **Fitzwilliams** impaling ? : quarterly, in the first quarter, a fleur-de-lys. **N.B.** In the 1970 restoration this shield was painted over and now bears: Quarterly, azure and or, in the first quarter a fleur-de-lys of the second.

5. **Fitzwilliams** quartering **Warenne** impaling **Cromwell**: Argent, a chief gules, overall a bend azure; **Tatshall**:Chequy or and gules, a chief ermine; **Barnake**: Ermine, a fess gules; **Driby of Tattershall**; **Albini**: Gules, a lion rampant or; **Meschins, Earl of Chester**: Azure, three garbs or; **Lupus, Earl of Chester**: Azure, a wolf's head erased argent.

On the inscription is a shield bearing: **Fitzwilliams**; **Warenne**; **Cromwell**; **Tatshall**; **Barnake**; **Driby of Tatteshall**; **Albini**; **Meschines**; **Lupus**; **Green of Drayton, Northants.**: Argent, a cross engrailed gules; **Warenne**; **Roos**: Azure, three water bougets argent; **Rochford**: Quarterly or and gules a bordure bezanty; ? : Gules, an eagle displayed or; **Fitzwilliams**. In the eighth quarter, an annulet for difference impaling **Sackville**: Quarterly or and gules, overall a bend vair.

On the 1674 restoration plate are two shields bearing:

1. **Fitzwilliams** impaling **Perry alias Hunter**: Argent, on a chevron azure, three bugle horns or, between three lions rampant gules;

2. **Fitzwilliams** impaling **Cremer**: Argent, three wolves' heads erased sable, on a chief gules as many cinquefoils pierced or.

The British Museum has the top half of a military figure in a tabard, the head lost, which is probably the upper half of Sir William. In 1854, J.G.Waller reported in the Archaeological Journal that this had been bought in London for the Museum.   It disappeared for a time after air raids in 1940, but has since been found.   Norris suggests this part was removed at the restoration as the head was already gone and the whole renewed. It bears the quartered shield as on the inscription.

The family claims to be one of the country's oldest, coming over with the Conqueror. William Fitzwilliams was born about 1460 and bought the Manor of Marholm in 1502. A prominent merchant, he served as Treasurer and Chamberlain to Cardinal Wolsey. He was married three times. One of his daughters can be seen on a brass at Deene, Northants.(M.S.II) and another on a brass at Clapham, Sussex (M.S.V). He died in London, but was buried at Marholm. On the way north the cortege was involved in a riot at Hoddesdon, later the subject of a lengthy lawsuit.

2. CROSS AND LOMBARDIC MARGINAL INSCRIPTION, ROGER DE LA HIDE, 13th CENTURY, IN THE CHURCHYARD.

Noted by the Victoria County History in 1906 in its present position on the north side of the tower, the slab seems to have disappeared until the summer of 1923 when it was re-discovered. The remaining part shows the indent of a stem rising from a mound with this inscription round the edge:

....NUR . LE . V . MESIRE : ROGER : DE . LA . HIDE...

A Roger de la Hide owned the Manor of Marholm during the reign of Henry III.

3. INDENT OF INSCRIPTION

4. BRASS TO JOHN WHITTLEBURY, 1400.

This is noted by Simpson without any further information.

MAXEY

1. INDENT OF DEMI-EFFIGY OF PRIEST, INSCRIPTION, c1450, NORTH CHAPEL.

A simple indent to a priest.

2. INDENT OF LADY BETWEEN TWO CIVILIANS, FOOT INSCRIPTION, c1450, NORTH CHAPEL.

This worn indent is on a slab appropriated for a later inscription.

3. INDENT OF MILITARY, WIFE, CANOPY, SHIELDS, c1500, NORTH CHAPEL.

The indent of a man in armour, wife in long dress and pedimental headdress, under a double canopy. The lower part of the slab seems to be cut away and probably contained the indents of children and two more shields.

4. OTHER BRASSES

Simpson notes some other brasses, which are unlikely to have been in this church.

a. John de Bykys, a cross flory c1360. **b.** A lady unknown 1474 and another dated 1402 **c.** The remainder hid.

MOLESWORTH

1. INDENT OF LOMBARDIC MARGINAL INSCRIPTION, NAVE.

In the Nave towards the west end is a worn and cracked tapering slab with a marginal inscription to the wife of (Walter?) DE MOLESWORTH. It is now largely illegible. More of the inscription is recorded in a drawing at the Norris Library and Museum dated 1894.

FEMME : WAL... : DE : MOLESWORTHE : GIST : ICI : DEU : DE : SALME : EIT

2. LOMBARDIC MARGINAL INSCRIPTION, NOW UNDER PULPIT.

The same source shows an identical slab now said to be under the floor and pulpit. Probably to Alinore de Molesworthe, mother of No.1. The inscription read:

ALI...E : MERE : W.....R : DE : MOLESWORTHE : GIST : ICI : DE : SA : ALME : EIT : MERCI

OFFORD D'ARCY

1. SIR LAURENCE PABENHAM, IN ARMOUR, TWO WIVES, ELIZABETH AND JOAN, FOOT INSCRIPTION; LOWER PART OF EFFIGIES POSSIBLY LOST, c1440, NAVE, (M.S.I).

The brass shows the figure of a man in plate armour between two wives. One wears a wide sleeved kirtle and the other a kirtle with tight fitting cuffs. Both have horned head-dresses. The inscription reads:

Hic jacent Laurencii Pabenham Miles qui obiit x die Mens' Junii a Dni MCCCC et Dna Elizabeth uxor dicti Laurencii / Una triu Soror' ac ffiliaru ac heredu dni Johis Engeyne dni de Engeyne que obiit xxiii die Mensis Septembr' Anno / Dni MCCCLXXVII ac dna Johanna scda ux dicti Laurencii filia Egidii Dawbeny Militis q'r' aiabz ppiciet ds Amen

A London Series B brass, the two female figures are palimpsest, one discovered in 1915 and the other in 1979. Both the reverses have canopy work showing the engraver's centre line down the middle - a most unusual feature. As the brass was obviously not completed it is likely that a mistake was made elsewhere in the engraving.

Clements saw the brass on the floor at the upper end of the south aisle, but for many years it was fixed to the south wall under the window. It was removed for cleaning and repair in the Egan workshop and in March 1981 set in a new stone slab in the Nave floor.

2.   WILLIAM TAYLARD, ECCLESIASTIC; INSCRIPTION, SCROLL, RELIGIOUS SYMBOL, SHIELD LOST, c1530, NAVE, (M.S.II).

This brass to an ecclesiastic in a cap, tippet, gown and hood was made in Cambridge. It has had a chequered history as the slab was formerly in the Chancel, but removed during a 19th Century restoration to the Tower floor. The brass itself became loose and was borrowed by a gentleman for a lecture in Huntingdon prior to 1890. He failed to return it to the churchwarden as in 1894, the Rev.H.Vicars heard of it lying thrown aside in a bakehouse. He bought the brass and fixed it to the wall of All Saints, huntingdon. It was returned shortly before the First World War and was loose again by 1979. The plate was repaired by the Egan workshop and re-fixed in the original slab in the Nave.

William Taylard was the son of William Taylard who can be seen on the earliest brass at Diddington. He was a pluralist of some note and held livings at Eynesbury, Abbot's Ripton, Offord D'Arcy, Irthlingborough, Huntingdon All Saints, St John's Hospital, Huntingdon and Stathum, Lincs. He died in 1532 and asked in his will "to be buryede in the myddis of the Chancel of Offorde".

3.   INSCRIPTION, JOHN ATKINSON, NOW LOST.

This was noted by Astry, Valpy French and Clements (who saw it in the Chancel). It read:

Johannes Atkinson dudum / Offordi Rector utriusque / Pius prudens vigilans fidelis / Anno aetatis climacterico / Christo milleno sexcenteno / Quarto que deno Junii septimo / Vitam hanc morte vel magis vita / Faeliciore commutavit / Istoque est conditus monumento / Quod illi posuit sumptu suo / Amans amanti conjux viro.

4.   INDENT OF INSCRIPTION PLATE, NOW LOST.

This is noted by the VCH and cannot now be traced. It was probably the indent of the Atkinson brass.

5.   TWO INDENTS OF CROSSES WITH HALF-EFFIGIES, NOW LOST.

The only reference to these is by Haines and, if they ever existed, may have been lost at the restoration.

6.   BRASS TO CIVILIAN, WIFE, c1490.

There is a reference to this by Simpson (not noted for his

accuracy). The Ecclesiastical and Architectural Topography 1851 mentions two civilians dated between 1480-1490, one of which may have been this brass.

7. BRASS TO CIVILIAN, c1480, NOW LOST.

The only reference is in Eccles. and Arch. Topography, 1851.

Note on re-fixing

In 1981 both the brasses were re-fixed. 1. The indent is prepared by cleaning, chipping off the previous mastic and digging out the lead holding the old rivets; 2. New and deeper rivet holes are drilled; 3. An angled hole is made to provide a key; 4. The new holes are cleaned by blowing air down them; 5. The indent is coated with a waterproof mastic; 6. The brass, to which new rivets in the form of hexagonal headed brass bolts have been fixed, is wire brushed to provide a key; 7. The back of the brass is coated with mastic; 8. A mixture of inert resin and dry sand is poured into the holes; 9. The two parts are now ready for fixing; 10. The brass is lowered into the indent; 11. The brass is held down until the resin has set. Mastic which has oozed out round the edges is cleaned off with parafin and the completed brass left for a fortnight while the resin hardens completely.

ORTON WATERVILLE

1. INSCRIPTION, JOHN DE HERLYNGTON, 1408; SHIELD LOST, NORTH AISLE, (M.S.I).

The inscription reads:

Hic jacet Johes de Herlyngton qui obiit / xii die Januarii A Dni Millmo CCCCVIII

2. INDENT OF INSCRIPTION PLATE, CHANCEL.

On a Purbeck slab in the Chancel.

3. RIVETS

There are some rivets in a step to the Chancel.

PASTON

1. CROSS AND INSCRIPTION, ROBERT DE MYTHING, NOW LOST.

Noted by Bridges, it was lost by the time Sweeting visited in the 18th Century. There was a cross flory of brass and a marginal inscription probably incised in the stone, which read:

Hic jacet Robertus de Mythinggiski quondam rector istius ecclesie cujus anime propitietur Deus.

PETERBOROUGH CATHEDRAL

Like most cathedrals, Peterborough was rich in brasses, many of its abbots and clergy being commemorated by magnificent memorials. In his book on the Cathedral, published in 1686, Gunton gives a graphic description of the destruction which he probably saw.

"On April 18th 1643 ... came the Parliament Forces to Peterborough ... they fell to execute their fury upon the Cathedral ... defacing the monuments, tearing the brass from the gravestones ... their Commanders of whom Cromwell was one, if not acting, yet not restraining the soldiers in the heat of their fury ... sculptures and inscriptions in brass, these they force and tear off. So that whereas there were many fair pieces of this kind before, as that of Abbot Wm. de Ramsey, whose large marble gravestone was plated over with brass and several others the like. There is not much now".

Fortunately Gunton described many of those which were destroyed.

Even more fortuitously Dugdale foresaw what might happen. In the British Library is a book of drawings owned by the Earl of Winchilsea and Nottingham. The preface to this unpublished work comments: "the said Mr Dugdale, therefore received encouragement from Sir Christopher Hatton, then a member of the House of Commons (who timely foresaw the approaching storm) in summer Anno 1641 having with him Mr Wm Sedgewick (a skilful Arms Painter) repair'd first to St Paul's...and there made exact Draughts of all the monuments...copying the epitaphs according to the very letter...and having done so rode to Peterborough". The drawings are reproduced here.

Further losses took place in the Victorian times when the Cathedral was restored, especially its paving. Minor losses have taken place since the First World War. Nevertheless, from different sources a remarkably complete picture of the Cathedral's brasses emerges.

1. INSCRIPTION; SHIELD LOST, QUEEN CATHARINE OF ARAGON, 1536, RELAID, NORTH CHOIR AISLE.

The only brass remaining in the Cathedral is this mutilated and almost illegible inscription to the first wife of Henry VIII. In 1779 the monument was noted as being upon the steps adjoining the door opening from the North Aisle near the east end into the choir. Near it is a stone with the indent of a brass shield in a lozenge compartment. Jerome Bertram suggests the inscription may be late 18th Century. The first note of it was in 1830 by William Cobbett, but it could well have been missed by earlier visitors. The inscription reads:

Queen Catharine AD MDXXXVI

2.   INDENT OF CROSS, LOMBARDIC MARGINAL INSCRIPTION,   c1320,
SOUTH TRANSEPT CHAPEL.

In St Oswald's Chapel this grey marble slab has a cross,   probably
incised and not containing an inlay.   The marginal inscription   is
in separate Lombardic letters and what can be deciphered reads:

(HIC) IAC/E(T)...U...IS : ISTI / US : MONAST / ERII..

One brass stop still remains (1984). An outer strip on each side
was powdered with what were apparently brass roses or quartrefoils,
now lost.

3.   INDENT OF ABBOT, CANOPY, TWO SHIELDS, LOMBARDIC MARGINAL
INSCRIPTION,   ABBOT GODFREY DE CROYLAND, 1329, NOW IN NORTH CHOIR
AISLE.

This was one of the brasses lost during the Civil War, but both the
slab and Dugdale's drawing survive. It shows a bareheaded Abbot,
holding a crozier and a book, standing on a lion beneath a canopy.
Between the pinnacles are two shields bearing:

Peterborough Abbey: Gules,   two keys in saltire between four
crosses formee fitchee or

England: Gules, three lions passant guardant or.

Of the inscription in separate Lombardic letters, a stop and the
letter "V" survived till the 20th Century, but could not be found
in 1984.   The inscription is:

DE : CROI/LAUND : NATUS : JACET : HIC : GODEFRI/DUS :
HUMATUS : / BURGI : PRELATUS : CUI : SOLVAS : CHRISTE :
/ REATUS :

Across the top of the slab between the canopy pinnacles   is the
final word of the inscription: **AMEN**

4.   INDENT OF CROSS WITH MARGINAL INSCRIPTION, c1360, NORTH CHOIR
AISLE.

The remains of a fine cross with a marginal inscription with
quartrefoils at the corners.

5.   INDENT OF CANOPY, THREE SHIELDS, REMAINDER OF SLAB LOST,
SOUTH AISLE.

Almost certainly the remains of the brass to Abbot John Depinge,

1439, which was formerly near No.3 and lost in 1643. Dugdale's drawing shows an abbot with mitre and crozier standing under a triple canopy. Four shields are depicted:

1. **See of Westminster** (incorrectly drawn): a cross flory between four birds

2. **England and France quarterly**

3. **Peterborough Abbey**

4. **As 1.**

There was a foot inscription which read:

Orate pro anima dni Johis Depinge quondam Abbatis hujus Monasterii, qui obiit V die Decembris A Dni Mill CCCCXXIX.

6. INDENT OF MILITARY, WIFE, FOUR SHIELDS, 18 SMALL PLATES, c1500, PORCH.

7. INDENT OF PLATE, INSCRIPTION, PORCH.

8. INDENT OF INSCRIPTION, REMAINDER OF SLAB COVERED, NORTH CHOIR AISLE.

9. INDENT OF INSCRIPTION, PORCH.

10. INDENT OF INSCRIPTION, PORCH.

11. INDENT OF INSCRIPTION, NORTH CHOIR AISLE.

12. INDENT OF INSCRIPTION, NORTH CHOIR AISLE.

13. INDENT OF INSCRIPTION, OUTSIDE.

There is the indent of an inscription in the arcade north of the entrance porch.

14. INDENT OF LOMBARDIC MARGINAL INSCRIPTION, UDEAL DE ALWALTON, NOW LOST (?), c1320.

An illustration of this curious slab, which cannot now be traced, shows an inscription in separate letters reading:

HIC JA/CET WDE/AL / WALTONA

15. INDENT OF CROSS, PARTLY INCISED, PARTLY INLAID, SHIELD c1330, NOW LOST.

A cross with a stepped base, stem and shield of arms, probably inlaid with brass. The ends of the cross were apparently incised and above it may be the indent of an inscription. Formerly in the Porch.

16. INDENT OF CROSS, LOMBARDIC MARGINAL INSCRIPTION, ESTRANGE DE WATERVILLE, c1330, NOW LOST.

This existed in 1868 but has now gone. Dugdale's drawing shows a fine floriated cross in the Nave. The inscription read:

W : S/KI : PAR : CI : PASSEZ : PUR : LE : ALME : ESTRAUNGE : DE : WATERVILLE : PRIEZ

17. INDENT OF CROSS, LOMBARDIC MARGINAL INSCRIPTION, ROBERT DE SUTTON, c1330, NOW LOST.

Brown Willis records this as being in the Lady Chapel and Dugdale illustrates it. The inscription read:

ICY GIST THOMAS LE FITZ ROBERT DE SUTTON : PATER NOSTER PUR L'ALME IUR CRESSINES.

18. INDENT OF CROSS, LOMBARDIC MARGINAL INSCRIPTION, JOHN DE THINGHAM, c1330, NOW LOST.

Dugdale draws this fine cross flory near the choir door and both he and Brown Willis provide this separate letter inlay inscription:

HIC : JACET : JOHANNES : DE : THINGHAM : PRIOR : ISTIUS : LOCI : CUIUS : ANIME : PROPITIETUR : DEUS : AMEN

19. INDENT OF CROSS, LOMBARDIC MARGINAL INSCRIPTION, WILLIAM PARYS, c1330, NOW LOST.

Illustrated by Dugdale and recorded by Brown Willis, the inscription read:

HIC : JACET : WILLS : PARYS : QUONDAM : PRIOR : BURGI : CUJUS : ANIME : MISEREATUR : DEUS : AMEN : PATER : NOSTER : AVE : MARIA

20. MILITARY FIGURE, INDENT OF CANOPY AND LOMBARDIC MARGINAL INSCRIPTION, SIR EDMUND GASCELIN, c1330, NOW LOST.

Dugdale's drawing of this remarkable brass shows an early chain mailed knight of which only a dozen or so similar brasses or illustrations remain. Formerly in the Nave, it may have existed until Brown Willis' time and portrays a man in complete chain mail covered by a surcoat. The shield bears: seven billets, a label for difference. The canopy was gone when the drawing was made. The inscription, in separate Lombardic letters was:

CY : GIST : EDMUND : GASCELIN : SEYNUR : DE : MARHAM :

JADIS : DE : RI : ALME : DIEU : EIT : MERCI : PATER :
NOSTER

He was apparently the second husband of Lady Isabella de Waterville of Marholm.

21. CROSS FROM TABERNACLE, CROZIER, BUST, MARGINAL INSCRIPTION, ABBOT ADAM DE BOOTHBY, 1338, NOW LOST.

Dugdale's drawing of this curious brass shows it between the choir and the great altar. The inscription read:

Claustri praelatus hujus cubat hic vocitatus Adam qui natus
erat Boothby, nece stratus; Vir castus, justus, omni
virtute robustus / ....M. Semel, X trina, ter et sex i
quoque; bina Pars donetur ei celestis nunc requiei.

22. CIVILIAN, CANOPY, ENTABLATURE, TWO SHIELDS, MARGINAL INSCRIPTION, ROBERT DE THORPE, 1372, NOW LOST.

A fine brass to the Chancellor of Edward III, the figure is shown with the head resting on a cushion. He wears a long tunic with the hood folded back on the shoulders. It was formerly at the upper end of the Nave. The inscription, from various sources read:

Hic jacet tumulatus Dominus Robertus de Thorpe, Miles quondam
Cancellarius Domini Regis Anglie qui obiit vicesimo nono die
Junii Anno Domini Millesimo tricentesimo .... septuagesimo
secundo cujus anime propitietur Deus Amen

23. INDENT OF SHIELD, MARGINAL INSCRIPTION, SON OF WILLIAM DE THORPE, 1375, NOW LOST.

Dugdale supplies the drawing which is recorded as brass by Thynne. The inscription from Brown Willis read:

Hic jacet ... miles filius Domini Wilhelmi de Thorpe; qui
moriebatur apud Towton Watervile die Jovis· decimo die Augusti
Anno Domini Millessimo CCCLXXV cujus anime propitietur Deus.

24. CIVILIAN, FOOT INSCRIPTION, JOHN DE HARWEDON, c1400, NOW LOST.

Formally at the upper end of the South Aisle was the figure of a man in civil dress - a long tunic and cloak. The inscription read:

Hic jacet Johannes de Harwedon quondam Seneschallus Burgi:
cujus anime propitietur Deus Amen.

25. ABBOT, CANOPY, TWO SHIELDS, FOOT INSCRIPTION, WILLIAM GENGE, 1408, NOW LOST.

Dugdale has a drawing of Abbot Genge standing under a single canopy between the pediments of which were two shields bearing:

1. England and France quarterly

·2. Peterborough Abbey

The inscription read:

> Prudens praelatus Willelmus Genge vocitatus Primus mitratus Abbas, jacet hic tumulatus. Summe vivebat claustrum Summeque; regebat Mundum spernebat que fecerat illa docebat : Vixerat ornatus virtutibus immaculatus. Tonsus quadratus tempatus et igne probatus Annis vissensis Burgum rexit bene plenis careat penis precibus potiamur amenis.

26. INSCRIPTION, WILLIAM EXTON, NOW LOST.

In the South Choir Aisle was an inscription recorded by Gunton and Brown Willis which read:

> Hic Wilihelmus erat Prior Exton, Philosophator Nobilis exgenere generis quoque nobilitator....

27. CIVILIAN, WIFE, SEVEN SONS, FOUR DAUGHTERS, FOOT INSCRIPTION, WILLIAM AND JOAN RAMSEY, 1489, NOW LOST.

Dugdale has the drawing of a man in a long tunic with a gypciere and rosary hanging from his belt. His wife wears an early pedimental head-dress. The sons are shown dressed similarly to their father while two of the daughters have butterfly head-dresses. The inscription read:

> Siste gradum, mortale meum spectare sepulchrum, Hic ego qui jaceo num genus ecce tuum; Fratris Wilhelmi Ramsey Venerabilis olim istius Abbatis hic in honore loci Petriburgh Bayly, Kyllum vocor ipse Johannes; Mecum sponsa jacet ecce Johanna mea. Mihi sunt nati, mihi sunt nateque Puelle, Willmus, Thomas, Willma et ipse Johannes, Walterus, Richardus, Thomas, Agnes, mihi Marga, Gratia sit proles, et Caterina, mea. Orate precor ut Deus salvet nos omnes ab inferno, Jactus fuit en lapis iste 1489, April 19.

28. ABBOT, CANOPY WITH SIDE NICHES, TABERNACLE, ONE SHIELD, THREE OTHERS LOST, MARGINAL INSCRIPTION, WILLIAM DE RAMSEY, 1496, NOW LOST.

Dugdale's drawing shows what must have been the finest brass in the Cathedral. Abbot Ramsey is portrayed in full vestments with crozier and mitre. It was at the upper end of the Nave. In the canopy niches were saints: **Dexter** - St Peter, St Andrew, St James the Great, St John the Evangelist; **Sinister** - St Jude, St Thomas,

St James the Less. The sole remaining shield bore a rebus (an heraldic pun): a ram, the word sey and the letter W. The marginal inscription read:

Abbus Burgensis Willelmus ut hic tumulatus Ramisey natus, praelatus jam nece stratus. En qui protrusis rodendus vermibus instant Vir prudens, justus, pius, omnibus et honorandus, Custos, benignus, omni virtute decorus, Corde Suo statuit nunquam offendare Christum Cortigans rigidos, tractans pietate modestos, Debita persolvi et diruta multa novari. Praestet plena suis stipendia jam cenebitis, et propter missas celebrandus cotidianus Ipse monasterio semper servabat honorem Pax donetur ei....

29. INSCRIPTION, MARIA AUSTIN, 1673, NOW LOST.

In the Nave was a brass whose inscription was noted by Brown Willis as:

Maria uxor charissima Humfridi Austin, hujus Ecclesiae quondam Praecentoris, Vitam hanc meliore mutavit Jun 4, Aetat. 50 Anno Domini 1673.

30. CIVILIAN, WIFE, THREE SONS, DAUGHTERS LOST, FOOT INSCRIPTION, WILLIAM AND ALICE SMITH, 1516, ALL NOW LOST.

Dugdale's drawing shows a civilian in a long fur lined gown with a gypciere and rosary. His wife also has a rosary. Formerly in the Nave, the inscription read:

Pray for the soules of William Smyth and Alice his wife / which William decessed the XX day of Jun. ye yere of our / Lord MDXVI on whose soul Jesu have mercy.

31. INSCRIPTION, SIMON ENGLISH, 1592, NOW LOST.

Formerly in the Lady Chapel was this brass to, according to Gunton, a school master, which read:

Simoni English Archididascalo Petriburghi celeberrimo Epiphaniae die Anno Domini 1592 mortuo Discipulus Thomas Green Hieronymi filius Gratitudinis ergo posuit.

32. CIVILIAN, WIFE, NOW LOST.

Bloxam notes the figure of a civilian and wife apparently of the 15th Century in the Porch.

33. INSCRIPTION, BISHOP JOHN CHAMBERS, 1556, NOW LOST.

Gunton saw this chamfer inscription round a marble monument:

Credo quod redemptor meus vivit et in novissimo die de terra
surrecturus sum et in carne mea videbo Deum salvatorem meum :
reposita est haec spes mea in sinu meo Moritur die...   Anno
Domini Millesimo Quingentesimo Tricesimo.

34. INSCRIPTION, HUMPHREY AUSTIN, 1668, NOW LOST.

Noted by Brown Willis this inscription read:

HIC JACET HUMFRIDUS AUSTIN / HUJUS ECCLESIE CAN / ONICUS
PRECENTOR / ET / CANTORUM / MAGISTER QUI AB HOC TER / RESTI
AD COELEST / EM CHORUM / MIGRAVIT JUN / XI AN DOM MCCLXVII
AET LXIII / Charrissimo conjugi posuit Maria Austin.

35. INSCRIPTION, ELIZABETH PARKER, 1663, NOW LOST.

Recorded in a c1731 British Library manuscript is this brass on a
grey marble slab which read:

HERE LYETH INTER'D THE / BODY OF ELIZABETH THE / WIFE OF
LAWRENCE PARKER / WOAD MERCHANT WHO / DEPARTED THIS LIFE /
JULY 6, 1663 / WELL MAY HER HUSBAND CEASE HIS TEARS / FOR SHE
BUT SLEEPS TILL CHRIST APPEARS.

36. THREE SONS, SIX DAUGHTERS, FOUR SHIELDS; INDENTS OF CIVILIAN, WIFE, FOOT INSCRIPTION, c1490, ALL NOW LOST.

Dugdale's drawing shows the indents of two figures, with four
shields each bearing: a chevron between three roses quartering
three wheat-sheaves.

37. INDENT OF CIVILIAN, WIFE, CHILDREN, PORCH, NOW LOST.

Bloxam noted this indent about 1862.

38. INDENT OF BISHOP, FOOT INSCRIPTION, FOUR QUARTREFOILS, MARGINAL INSCRIPTION, NOW LOST.

Dugdale has a drawing of this indent on an altar tomb in St Mary's
Chapel.

39. INDENTS OF LOMBARDIC MARGINAL INSCRIPTIONS, NOW LOST.

Beloe noted (c1899) three or four (other than Croyland and Waltona)
separate letter inlay Lombardic inscriptions. Brown Willis
recorded an ancient marble which had an inscription round the verge
now illegible and defaced.....appropriated to R.Slye 1660. This
may not have been a brass inlay inscription.

40. INDENTS OF INSCRIPTIONS.

Brown Willis noted two slabs in the Nave with inscription indents.

41. INDENTS.

Brown Willis noted 'several other figures and inscriptions'.

42. INDENTS.

The VCH in 1906 recorded a number of stones with indents of brasses in the Porch. These are probably those still remaining.

43. BRASSES

In 1635 Lt. Hammond, a Lieutenant of the Military Company in Norwich visited the Cathedral and noted three brasses in the porch:

a. On the porch floor b. Mural in the Porch c. The brass of Prelate Adams

PETERBOROUGH MUSEUM

1. LADY, c1430, (M.S.I).

This London Series B figure is one of the wives from the brass to John Pedder, the remains of whose memorial is in Dunstable Church, Beds. (M.S.II).

2. TWO CHILDREN, A BOY AND A GIRL, c1463, (M.S.II).

The two figures, on one plate, are from an unknown church.

RAMSEY

1. INDENT OF CROSS, MARGINAL INSCRIPTION, c1350, SOUTH AISLE.

This is covered almost completely by the organ and what can be seen of the slab is worn and damaged. The coffin shaped stone bears the indent of a brass or marble inlay with a deep border at the sides.

2. BRASS NOW LOST.

Clements records, on the South wall of the Chancel, a brass with the word **RESURGEM** on it. In 1673 Prebendary Robins asked in his will for this word to be cut upon a stone close to his grave and this is now on the wall outside the Chancel. It may be that the word was engraved on brass and fixed to the inside as well.

3. INDENT OF CROSS, LOMBARDIC MARGINAL INSCRIPTION, NOW LOST.

This is given by Sweeting without any further details.

4. SEVERAL INDENTS.

Brayley and Britton note several large slabs in the Nave which were inlaid with brasses, most probably of abbots and priests of Ramsey.

5. BRASS.

It has been suggested that the brass to the last Abbot of Ramsey, John Lawrence, now in Burwell Church, Cambs. (M.S.I), was originally made for Ramsey, but laid at Burwell following the dissolution of the monasteries.

ST IVES

1. INDENT OF CROSS, INSCRIPTION, 15TH CENTURY, NAVE.

At the North-east corner of the Nave lies a slab with the indent of a Latin cross with a thin stem. The cross ends in a fleur de lys. An inscription plate, probably of a later date, has been let into the stone across the stem, but is now lost. All very worn.

2. INDENT OF MILITARY, TWO WIVES, FOOT INSCRIPTION, c1460, NAVE.

Now very worn, the indent is on an appropriated slab.

ST NEOTS

1. INDENT OF CROSS, FOUR SHIELDS, LOMBARDIC MARGINAL INSCRIPTION, JOAN LA GOUSLE, c1320, NORTH CHANCEL AISLE.

Hidden behind the organ is a worn and almost illegible slab. It was formerly in the passage between the north and south porches. Two illustrations of it have been printed which differ slightly. The earlier, by Gough, has been reproduced as the dog at the base of the cross can be seen clearly. An 1851 reference suggests more of the brass remained at that time. The inscription reads:

JOHANE . LA . GOUSLE . GIST . ISSI . PRIE . PUR . LE . ALME . DE LUY . KY . PUR . LALME . DE . LUY . PRIERA . CENT . JOURS . DE . PARDOUN . AVERA .

2. BRASS TO THOMAS LYNDE AND HIS TWO WIVES, ALICE AND JOAN, 1527, NOW LOST.

The College of Arms Visitation for 1684 notes a brass to Thomas Lynde in the dress of a Yeoman of the Guard with a poleaxe, a rose on his breast and a crown on his left shoulder. The inscription was taken off and remained with the Sexton. There were four roses (or quartrefoils) at each corner, but no arms. Gorham says the brass was in the North Aisle and gives this inscription:

Of yor charite py for ye soules of Thoas Lynde late Yoman of

ye Crowne to oe Soueayne Lorde Kyng Henry ye VIIIth: Alice
and Johanne his wyves: whych Thos. deceasyd the xxii day of
Meche ye yere of oe Lord MCCCCCXXVII.

3.   BRASS TO SIR ROBERT PAYNE, 1621, NOW LOST.

Gorham recorded this in the centre of the pavement of the Jesus
Chapel c1732 with the figures of a knight and a lady.   At the head
were two shields bearing:

1. **Payne:** Azure, a bend raguly between six etoiles or

2. **Payne** impaling **Rotherham:**   Vert, three stags trippant or.

The inscription read:

> HERE LIES INTERRED THE BODY OF SIR ROBERT PAYNE / KNIGHT,
> DECEASED THE 18TH DAY OF JUNE A DNI 1631, AGED / 58 YEARS:WHO
> MARRYED ELIZABETH THE DAUGHTER OF / GEORGE ROTHERHAM OF
> SOMERIS IN COM. BEDFORD ESQ : BY / WHOME HE HAD ISSUE 5
> SONNS AND 6 DAUGHTERS. / THIS MOURNING VAULT OF DEATH, THAT
> MUST ATTAYNE / AS PLEDGE AWHILE THE DUST OF HONOURED PAYNE /
> IS BUT HIS TOMBE, NOR CAN IT STYLED BE / A MONUMENT OF HIM,
> HIS MEMORIE / AND FAME ON EARTH WITH THOSE GOOD DEEDS HE SENT
> / TO HEAVEN BEFORE HIM, ARE HIS MONUMENT. / THE COUNTRY'S
> TEARS, FARR BETTER THAN THIS STONE / WILL TELL THE READER
> NOBLE PAYNE IS GONE / ASK THEM NOT MEE; THEY FEEL THE LOSS OF
> HIM / AND WILL FOR EVER KEEP HIS JUST ESTEEM

Sir Robert Payne was Sheriff of Cambridgeshire and Huntingdonshire
in 1607.

4.   INDENT OF THREE FIGURES, INSCRIPTION PLATE, FOUR ROUNDELS,
UNDER TOWER ARCH, NOW LOST.

In 1926, the RCHM described this as much worn.   In 1984 it could
not be traced.

5.   INDENTS, NOW LOST.

Gorham notes "many other brasses have perished".

6.   BRASS, POSSIBLY NOW LOST.

The undated church guide by Galley notes an older slab on the right
of No.1 and "there was mutilated brass in the middle which may be
under the organ".

7.   BRASS TO JOHN GISMAN, 1517.

In the Archdeaconry of Hunts. Wills is one by John Gisman or
Gesnam of St Neots, 1517 who directed his executors to buy a

gravestone with three images, the stone to be 6' long and 2'6"
wide. This may be No.4.

1. SIR WILLIAM MOYNE, IN ARMOUR, AND WIFE MARY; FOUR SHIELDS
AND MARGINAL INSCRIPTION NEARLY ALL LOST, 1404, MURAL IN CHANCEL,
(M.S.I).

This large London Series B brass was formerly on an Altar tomb in
the Chancel of the old church. It was moved to the new church in
1879 and laid on the floor below the bell rope, being moved to the
Chancel in 1905. A drawing by Gough in the Bodleian Library shows
the brass on an Altar Tomb and a rubbing from the same source has
more of the inscription. The Camden Visitation of 1613 noted the
brass on the south side of the Chancel and gave this inscription
(bracketed parts remaining):

> ...(Mense Aprilis Anno Domini MCCCCIIII et Maria Uxor ejus,
> quor'a)nimab' propiciet' deus Am(en)

Two shields were seen by the Visitation which may have belonged to
the indents of the slab. These bore:

1. Le Moyne: Argent, two bars sable, in chief three mullets sable

2. Le Moyne impaling ? : a lion rampant guardant within a bordure
engrailed.

The brass depicts a figure in mixed chain and plate armour, the
body mail protection being covered by a cloth or leather jupon with
a scalloped edge. Behind the head is the crest of the Le Moyne
family - a monk holding a flagellum. His wife wears a
particularly fine reticulated or caul head-dress, a tight fitting
dress and a mantle.

Sir William was probably born about 1338 and was heir to manorial
interests in various parts of the county. Present at the Battle
of Poitiers, he became Sheriff of Huntingdonshire and
Cambridgeshire in 1378/9. His wife, was a Hainaulter and
formerly in the service of Queen Philippa, wife of Edward III.
She was married four times - the last being to Sir William, and
died about 1411.

2. INSCRIPTION, MARY NEWTON, 1633, MURAL, CHANCEL, (M.S.I).

Prior to 1900 this was on a slab half overgrown with grass on the
site of the Chancel in the ruined church of St Andrew. Clements
records it at the entrance to the Chancel. It reads:

THE MEMORY OF THE JUST IS BLESSED 10 PRO 7 / HERE RESTETH YE
BODY OF MARY NEWTON / YE LATE FAITHFULL WIFE OF JOHN NEWTON /

RECTOR OF THIS CHURCH, WHO IN THE 32 / YEAR OF HER AGE, ON
YE 6 OF AUGUST IN YE / YEAR OF OR LORD GOD 1633 DEPARTED /
THIS LIFE IN YE TRUE FAYTH OF CHRIST, / IN MUCH PACIENCE &
COMFORT: / I AM DEAD & MY LIFE IS HID WITH CHRIST / IN GOD,
WHEN CHRIST WHO IS MY LIFE SHALL / APPEARE, THEN SHALL I ALSO
APPEAR / WITH HIM IN GLORY.

SOMERSHAM

**1. PRIEST; FOOT INSCRIPTION, FOUR ROUNDELS LOST, c1530,
CHANCEL, (M.S.I).**

Formerly in the centre of the chancel, this Suffolk engraved brass
is now against the North wall. It portrays a priest in mass vestments holding a chalice and wafer. Scratched on the brass are the
letters S.I.M.

**2. INDENT OF MILITARY, FIVE SHIELDS, FOOT INSCRIPTION,
PROBABLY RICHARD THWAYTES, 1467, NAVE.**

The slab, which Clements saw in the South Aisle, is now broken in
half and largely covered by the font. The figure disappeared
sometime after 1850 and the slab was complete until about 1890.
The indent shows a military figure with his feet resting on a
hound. There were five shields, one at each corner and one above
the head. An brass inscription, probably belonging to this
indent, is noted in several manuscripts:

Hic jacet Ricus Thwaytes Armiger quondam Marischallus Hospice
Dni Willmi Gray Eliensis Episcopi qui obiit quinto die mensis
Septembris A Dni 1467, cujus aie ppiciet Deus.

**3. INDENT OF PRIEST, FOUR SQUARES, FOOT INSCRIPTION, c1500,
CHANCEL.**

Formerly in the centre of the Chancel, this is now against the
South wall.

**4. INDENT OF PRIEST, FOUR COCKS AT CORNERS, FOOT INSCRIPTION,
c1530, SOUTH PORCH.**

Formerly in the Chancel, this worn slab probably commemorated John
Alcoke, Parson of Somersham (instituted 1488) who, in his will,
proved in 1525, asked to be buried in the Chancel.

5. INDENT OF RECTANGULAR PLATE AND INSCRIPTION, NAVE.

6. INDENT OF INSCRIPTION, NAVE.

SOUTHOE

1. INSCRIPTION, SIMON DE BURGH, 1395, NOW LOST.

A Harleian manuscript notes this as being on a gravestone in 1613 although it may not have been a brass.

2.   INDENT OF TWO FIGURES, TWO GROUPS OF CHILDREN,   INSCRIPTION, NOW LOST.

A note in the Norris Library and Museum records this indent in the SE corner of the churchyard almost covered by grass in 1939.   BY 1984 it was completely covered or lost.   The 1613 Visitation records an inscription to Edmond and Jane Hatley 1598, which may have belonged to this indent which Inskip Ladds suggests was late 16th Century.

SPALDWICK

1.   INDENT OF CIVILIAN, WIFE, INSCRIPTION, c1460, SOUTH CHAPEL.

Now very worn.

2.   INDENT OF FIGURE, SCROLL, INSCRIPTION, SOUTH CHAPEL.

Now very worn.

N.B.   In 1862 the whole of the floor was taken up and repaved.

STAMFORD BARON, ST MARTIN'S WITHOUT

1.   CROSS FLORY, INSCRIPTION, NOW LOST.

The Gentleman's Magazine for 1846 notes a coffin lid adorned with an elegant cross flory and inscription to John Petrian which may not have been brass.

STANGROUND

1.   INSCRIPTION, ROBERT SMITH, 1558, AND ALICE SMITH, 1595, MURAL CHANCEL, (M.S.I).

The inscription, which is probably from the Southwark workshop, reads:

> HIC JACET CORPUS ROBERTI SMITH GENOS / QUI OBIIT QUARTO DIE DECEMBRIS A DNI 1558 / FINIBZ EXIGUIS CLAUDUNTUR CORPORIS ARTUS / VIVA VIVET VIRTUS SPIRITUS ASTRA IENET. / HERE LYETH BURYED THE BODYE OF / ALICE SMITH WIFE TO THOMAS SMITH SONNE TO THE ABOVE SAID ROBT SMITH / WHO DYED THE VTH OF SEPTEMB A DNI 1595. / WHOSE CONSTANT ZEALE TO SERVE THE LORD / WHOSE LOYALL LOVE TO HUSBAND DERE / WHOSE TENDER CARE TOWARDS CHILDREN AL / EDM / REMAINES ALYVE THOUGH CORPES LYE HERE / SMITH.

The holes in this oddly shaped and rather battered brass indicates it was formerly elsewhere in the church. There were major restorations in in 1844 and 1858.

2. INSCRIPTION AND ACHIEVEMENT, ELIAS PETIT, 1634, MURAL IN CHANCEL, (M.S.II).

Two brass plates on the North wall of the Chancel. The upper plate has an achievement, which shows:

Petit: Argent, on a chevron gules between three lion's heads erased sable, crowned or, as many bezants quartering Daundelion: three lions rampant between two bars dancetty.

STEEPLE GIDDING

1. INDENT OF CIVILIAN, WIFE, c1520, NAVE.

A large slab in the centre of the Nave shows the indent of a civilian with long hair and a gown belted at the waist. His wife wears a pedimental head-dress.

2. INSCRIPTION, ANTHONY HILL, 1690, NOW LOST.

Clements records this brass on a freestone in the Chancel.

SUBTER HUNC LAPIDEM / IN NOVISSIMUM DIEM REPOSITAE / SUNT EXUVICAE ANTONY HILL M.A. / IN HAC ECCLESIA RECTORIS PER ANNOS / SEPTENDECEM PIETATIS ET BONORUM / OPERUM STUDIOSI QUI MORTI IMPORTUNAE / SUCCUBUIT DECIMO DIE FEBRUARII / ANNO DOMINI MILLESIMO SEXCENTESSIMO / NONOGESSIMO ET AETATIS SUAE QUADRAGESIMO NONO

STIBBINGTON

1. INSCRIPTION, JOHN HANGER, 1638, MURAL, CHANCEL.

On the south wall of the Chancel is this well polished inscription:

IN SPE RESURRECTIONIS / Hic obdormit Johannes Hanger, / Sacro-Sanctae Theologie Professor, / Annos huius Ecclesiae Rector. Natus Cantabrigiae 1579 sepulti' 1638 / VENI DOMINE JESU.

The Parish register records his marriage to Mary Smythe in 1611.

STILTON

1. CIVILIAN, WIFE, FOOT INSCRIPTION, RICHARD AND ANNE CURTHOYSE, 1606, NAVE, (M.S.I).

Standing on hassock-like pedestals, Richard wears a doublet and hose covered by a long gown with hanging false sleeves. His wife

has a stomacher, farthingale and a brimmed hat. There is the indent
of a small scroll above the figures. The inscription reads:

> HERE LYETH BURIED THE BODIES OF RICHARD CURTHOYSE / LATE OF
> STILTON YEOMAN AND ANNE HIS WIFE BY / WHOM SHE HAD ISSUE
> THREE SONES AND THREE DAUGHTERS / JOHN THO WILLIAM ANN
> ISABELL AND JOANE YE /SAID RICHARD DECEASED THE 15 DAY OF
> JANUARY / 1573 AND THE SAID ANN YE SECOND / OF DECEMBER ANNO
> 1606.

2. TWO CIVILIANS, FOOT INSCRIPTION, THOMAS AND JOHN CURTHOYSE,
1618, NAVE, (M.S.II).

On the same slab as their parents, the inscription notes that the
brass was provided by their brother William and the two memorials
may have been engraved together. All are from the Southwark
workshop of Bernard Johnson, possibly engraved with the help of the
master sculptor Nicholas Stone. It may be dated a little later
than 1618. The inscription reads:

> HERE ALSO LYETH BURIED THE BODIES OF THOMAS & / JOHN SONNES
> OF THE ABOVE SAID RICHARD AND ANN / WHICH THOMAS DECEASED THE
> XVII OF MAY / ANNO DOMINI 1590 AND JOHN THE XXII OF JULY /
> 1618 TO WHOSE PIOUS MEMORIE WILLIAM / HIS BROTHER CAUSED THIS
> MONUMENT / TO BE LAID.

SUTTON

1. INSCRIPTION AND ARMS, JOHN LOFTUS, 1657, NOW LOST.

A Cambridge University Library manuscript notes the arms as: a
chevron between three trefoils slipped. The inscription read:

> Here lyes ye body of John Loftus of Sutton sometime Lord of
> ye same Manour, who departed this life ye last of July A Dni
> 1657

Another Cambridge University Library manuscript suggests this brass
may once have been at Leighton Bromswold.

2. INDENT OF MAN, THREE WIVES, BRASS OF CHILDREN, NOW LOST

Baker notes Bridges: "at the upper end of the South Aisle is an
altar monument covered with marble on which were the portraits of a
man and his three wives and three children....torn off; but the
effigies of eight male and eight female children are left still
remaining".

THORNHAUGH

1. INDENT OF CROSS, LOMBARDIC MARGINAL INSCRIPTION, NAVE.

In the Nave is a cut down slab bearing the upper part of the indent of a cross. Round the edge is a marginal inscription, the remaining part reading:

PRIES PUR LALME .....PRIERA LE REFIST

THURNING

1. INSCRIPTION, SUSAN WELLS, 1658, (M.S.I).

Clements noted this on the south wall of the Chancel. It was removed to the Rectory when the church was restored and in 1896 was loose in the belfry. By 1919 it was mural in the Nave. It reads:

ADSPICE : DIC TITULUM, LEGIS IN HOC SEPULCHRO / CONIUGEM PAIM FAEMINAM RELIGIOSAM; / SUORUM NUPER SOLATIA IN FUNUS VERSA: / CLAUDITUR HIC AENIGMA CHARITATIS, SINE LIBERIS MATER; / QUOS ENIM NATURA MEGAVIT, FECIT CHARITAS, / QUAE IN HOC SALTEM DOMICILIO SEMPER INALVIT. MAIORA VELIS TEGITUR HAC URNA SUSANNA WELLES. / IMMO OSSA HIC CONDUNTUR, SPIRITUS IN SINU ABRAHE. / Reade here and learne to live. Under this stone / Lye Grace and Vertue twisted into one. / Here rests interr'd ye Friend (there needs no more) / of God, of Church, of Kindred, house and poore. / All would not save life, but here needs must lye / So much true worth, reade here and learn to dye. / Iter parentavit moestissimus Nepos. S.D.

TILBROOK

1. CIVILIAN, WIFE, INSCRIPTION, c1400, SOUTH AISLE.

'Now covered by the organ this fine brass portrays a civilian in a long fur-lined gown with a hood folded back round the neck. Hanging from his belt is a short sword known as an anelace. His wife also wears a long gown with her hair bound tightly to her head and covered with a scalloped cloth. It is a London Series A brass.

2. INSCRIPTION, JUDITH COOPER, 1741 AND OLIVER ST JOHN COOPER, 1781, MURAL, CHANCEL.

This well polished plate was made by S.Peacock whose name appears at the base. It reads:

IN MEMORY / OF / JUDITH THE WIFE OF THE / REVD OLR ST JOHN COOPER / WHO DIED 20TH OCTR. 1749 / AGED 31 YEARS / ALSO OF THE SAID REVD OLR / ST JOHN COOPER A.M. UPWDS / OF 43 YEARS RECTOR OF THIS / PARISH & 34 YEARS RECTOR / OF SHELTON. HE DIED 29TH / OCTR 1781 AGED 71 YEARS. / S.PEACOCK FECIT.

3. LOMBARDIC MARGINAL INSCRIPTION, SOUTH AISLE.

This early 14th Century slab is now almost illegible. The inscription is set between two parallel bands and may not be brass inlay.

4.   INSCRIPTION, JOHN CARTER, 1600, NOW LOST.

The only reference to this is by Haines who mentions a brass to John Carter and his wife, the former aet 67, the latter Agnes, daughter of Thomas Taylor of Lidlington; with sons John, Thomas and daughters Dorothy, Mary, Lucy, Penelope.

5.   INDENT OF INSCRIPTION, NOW LOST.

The Monumental Brass Society Transactions for 1891 lists the indent of a quadrangular plate with segments of circles projecting beyond the angles on the Tower floor.

UFFORD

1.   INDENT OF CIVILIAN, FOOT INSCRIPTION, TWO SMALL SHIELDS, c1460, CHANCEL.

The indent shows a figure in a long tunic, standing on a mound.

2.   INDENT OF THREE CHILDREN, FOOT INSCRIPTION, c1500, NORTH AISLE.

This monument to three children does not appear to have been have been part of a larger slab. The Victoria County History in 1906 noted the remains of an inscription on which the word "capellan" alone was legible.

UPWOOD

1.   INDENT OF DEMI-ECCLESIASTIC, INSCRIPTION, c1400, SOUTH AISLE.

The indent shows a priest in cope and almuce.

2.   INDENT OF LADY, FOUR SCROLLS, FOOT INSCRIPTION, c1470, SOUTH AISLE.

The indent shows a lady in a gown with a veil head-dress.

3.   INDENT OF RECTANGULAR PLATE, SOUTH AISLE.

A portion of slab bearing a square indent with a rivet hole in the centre, probably from a larger stone.

WARBOYS

1. RIVETS, SOUTH AISLE.

On the step from the South Aisle to the porch are a number of rivets.

2. BRASS TO ECCLESIASTIC, CANOPY LOST, NOW ALL LOST.

The only reference to this is by Brayley who writes "on a slab in the middle of the Nave, a full-length brass of a priest under the indent of a Gothic canopy, the inscription gone".

WENNINGTON

1. LOMBARDIC MARGINAL INSCRIPTION.

Bertram records that Stukeley's notes mention an inscription he found and he draws a coffin lid with Lombardic inscription, possibly not brass.

WINWICK

1. INSCRIPTION, EDWARD COLLINS, 1685, TOWER, (M.S.I).

On the Tower floor is a small plate reading:

> HERE LYETH THE BODY OF EDWARD COLLINS / THE SON OF EDWARD COLLINS OF WINWICK GEN / WHO DEPARTED THIS LIFE THE 28TH DAY OF JANUARY / 1685 IN THE 49TH YEAR OF HIS AGE AND LEFT / ISSUE EDMUND HIS ONLY CHILD

2. RIVETS.

Outside the South Porch is a broken stone bearing some rivets.

3. INSCRIPTION, JOHN SMITH, 1696, NOW LOST.

Clements notes a brass to a former rector which read:

> HIC JACET DEPOSITUM JOHANNIS SMYTH A M / ECCLESIE DE GIDDING MAGNA IN COM : HUNT : / INGDON VIGINTI NOVEMQZ ANNIS OCTOBZ MENSIBUS / VICARII : ET HUJUS ECCLESIAE VIGENTI SEXQZ / ANNIS SEPTEMQZ MENSIBUS CURATI. VIRI ECCLESIAE / ANGLICANE LELO VIR EXAEQUANDI CAPACITATE / ET FIDE MEMORIAE NITORE INGENII ET PRAECELLENTIA / DOCTRINAE VIX THEOLOGIS OPTIMUS ET MAXIMIS SECUNDI / OBIIT MIGENS VICCINIA DOLOR / DECIMO SEPTIMO DIE NOVEMBRIS ANNO / AERAE CHRISTIANAE 1696 AETATIS SUAE 61 / ACCUMBANT DUAE FILIAE MARIA ET FRANCISCA

WOODSTON

1. LOMBARDIC MARGINAL INSCRIPTION, HENRY DE IRTHLINGBURGH, NOW LOST.

Sweeting says this was written in the register by Rector Smyth as existing in his time (c1730). Possibly not brass, it was on a large freestone and read:

ORATE : P : ANIMA : FRATRIS : HENRICI : DE : IRTHLINGBURGH

WYTON

1. INSCRIPTION, JOHN FRANSHAM, NOW LOST.

The Astry manuscript records this inscription on brass:

Of your Charite pray for the soule of John Fransham and Margaret his wife on whose Souls Jesu have Mercy

The RCHM notes an indent in the churchyard (now in private possession) west of the west wall of the Nave showing the demi-effigies of a man and woman and inscription below. It assigns this to John Fransham.

2. BRASS, NOW LOST.

A note, probably dated about 1866, in the Norris Library and Museum records that "in preparing the Nave for new tiles a tombstone legendarily known as 'the Nun's Stone' containing a memorial brass was removed to the West end (exterior) of the church. Another stone with a brass was also removed to a similar position. Both brasses have now disappeared". In 1902 the 'Nun's Stone' which was formerly embellished with two brasses on the Chancel floor, was broken and shattered. The John Cole Manuscript lists three slabs - one with a man and two wives, probably this one; one with a man and wife, probably No.1; and No.3.

3. INDENT OF CIVILIAN, WIFE, FOOT INSCRIPTION, NOW LOST.

A drawing in the John Cole manuscript shows the figure of a man and a woman.

YAXLEY

1. INDENT OF FLORIATED CROSS WITH FIGURE IN HEAD, MARGINAL INSCRIPTION, c1370, NORTH CHOIR AISLE.

The remains of what must have been a fine and delicate brass to a priest. It now survives as a worn indent.

2. BRASSES ?

In the Architectural Association Sketch Book N.S.XII is drawing of Yaxley church c1840 which appears to show a marginal inscription with square corner plates and possibly a second indent, both in the Chancel.

BOOKS AND REFERENCES

H.Addington, 'Monumental Brasses in Bedfordshire Churches', Archaeological Journal, XL (1893), 303

Alcuin Club Collections VII

J.P.Anderson, The Book of British Topography (1881)

Anon, The Ecclesiastical and Architectural Topography of England, Part V (1845-55)

Anon, History of Great Gransden (1892)

The Antiquary, various volumes

Archaeological Journal, II, 306

Architectural Association Sketchbooks

S.Badham, J.Blair and R.Emmerson, Specimens of Lettering from English Monumental Brasses (1976)

G.Baker, The History and Antiquities of the County of Northampton (1822-41)

M.W.Barley, A Guide to British Topographical Collections (1974)

O.Barron, 'Our Oldest Families: the Fitzwilliams', Ancestor xii (1905), 111

G.B.Barrow, Genealogist's Guide, (1977)

Bedfordshire Central Library, Manuscript Church Notes (1823)

Bedfordshire County Record Office, various manuscripts

Bedfordshire Notes and Queries

C.M.Beloe, 'Notes on some Early Matrices in the Eastern Counties', Journal of the Oxford University Brass Rubbing Society, II (1900), 35

J.Bertram, Lost Brasses (1976)

J.Blair, 'English Monumental Brasses Before the Black Death', Collectanea Historica, Kent Archaeological Society (1981)

J.Elair, English Monumental Brasses Before the Black Death, typescript (1984)

M.H.Bloxam, A Glimpse of the Monumental Architecture of Gt. Britain (1834)

M.H.Bloxam, 'On the Effigies and Monumental Remains of Peterborough Cathedral', Archaeological Journal XIX (1862)

Bodleian Library, Oxford manuscripts: Gough 224; Gough Hunts 2; Gough Maps 12; MS Top. Gen. d.13; Ms Willis 38

C.A.Boutell, Christian Monuments in England and Wales (1854)

C.A.Boutell, A Series of Monumental Brasses of England (1849)

A.C.Bouquet, Church Brasses (1956)

E.W.Brayley and J.Britton, Beauties of England and Wales (1808)

J.C.Bridges, History and Antiquities of Northamptonshire (1762-91)

British Library manuscripts: Harleian 5329; 6127; Lansdowne 887; 919; 921; Add. Mss. 5806;

5830; 5834; 5836; 6763; 11,425; 16,967; 17,456; 18,481; 34,372; 37,179-80

J.Britton, Cathedral Antiquities V (1836)

J.P.Brooke-Little, Boutell's Heraldry (1950)

A.E.Bullock, Some Sculptural Works of Nicholas Stone (1908)

B.Burke, A General Armory (1884)

R.Busby, A Companion Guide to Brasses and Brass Rubbing, (1973)

Cambridge Collection of Rubbings

Cambridgeshire and Huntingdonshire Archaeological Society Transactions

Cambridgeshire County Libraries - local collections at Cambridge, Huntingdon, Peterborough

Cambridge University Library Manuscripts: 21; 741; 5352; Baker 36; 37

Camden Society, Visitation of Huntingdonshire 1613 (1849); Miscellany XVI (1936)

T.Candlin, Offord Cluny and Offord D'Arcy (1929)

T.Carruthers, History of Huntingdon (1824)

J.Carter, Ancient Architecture of England (1802)

W.Cobbett, Rural Rides (1853)

College of Arms, Visitation of Huntingdonshire, K.7.18

E.L.Cutts, Manual of Sepulchral Slabs (1849)

C.E.Dawes, The Parish Church of Colne (1891)

C.E.Dawes, Somersham: Past and Present (1890)

P.Dickinson, Barnack Church (1968)

H.Druitt, A Manual of Costume as Illustrated by Monumental Brasses (1906)

J.Dugdale, New British Traveller (1815)

C.Dunn, The Book of Huntingdon (1977)

B.Egan and M.Stutchfield, The Repair of Monumental Brasses (1981)

R.Emmerson, 'Monumental Brasses: London Design c1420-85', Journal, British Archaeological Association, CXXXI (1978), 50

D.H.Farmer, Oxford Dictionary of Saints (1978)

Fenland Notes and Queries

T.Fisher, Monumental Remains and Antiquities of Bedfordshire (1828)

R.Fox, History of Godmanchester (1831)

A.Fraser, Cromwell, Our Chief of Men (1975)

J.Franklyn, Brasses (1969)

V.French, 'Brasses of Huntingdonshire', Antiquary, IV (1881), 44, 115

W.E.Gawthorpe, The Brasses of Our Homeland Churches (1923)

G.L.Gomme, ed., Gentleman's Magazine Library: English Topography (1896)

G.C.Gorham, Eynesbury and St Neots (1824)

R.Gough, Sepulchral Monuments of Great Britain (1796)

F.J.Grant, Manual of Heraldry (1962)

S.Gunton, History of the Church of Peterborough (1686)

H.Haines, A Manual for the Study of Monumental Brasses (1848)

H.Haines, A Manual of Monumental Brasses (1861)

W.E.Hampton, Memorials of the Wars of the Roses (1979)

C.H.Hartshorne, The Sepulchral Remains in Northamptonshire (1840)

History Today, XXIX, 795

F.Hudson, The Brasses of Northamptonshire (1835)

C.R.Humphrey-Smith, ed., General Armory Two (1973)

Huntingdonshire Record Office, various sources

Anon, Huntingdonshire Historical Series (1902)

M.J.Karminkow, Genealogical Manuscripts in British Libraries (1967)

J.P.C.Kent, 'Monumental Brasses - A New Classification of Military Effigies', Journal, British Archaeological Association, 3rd Series XII (1949), 70

R.E.Latham, Revised Medieval Latin Wordlist (1965)

Leicestershire Architectural and Archaeological Society Transactions

R.Leach, An Investigation into the Use of Purbeck Marble in Medieval England (1978)

A.S.Lichliter, 700 Years of the Beville Family (1976)

G.Lipscomb, History and Antiquities of the County of Buckingham (1847)

H.W.Macklin, The Brasses of England (1907)

J.Mann, Monumental Brasses (1957)

C.R.Manning, A List of Monumental Brasses (1846) and C.G.R.Birch's annotated copy

G.W.Marshall, A List of the Monumental Brasses (1846)

A.L.Maycock, Nicholas Ferrar of Little Gidding (1933)

A.Mee, The King's England, Bedfordshire and Huntingdonshire (1973)

D.Meara, Victorian Monumental Brasses (1983) Monumental Brass Society, various Bulletins, Portfolios and Transactions

T.Moule, Biblioteca Heraldica (1822)

J.Nichols, History of Leicestershire (1795-1811)

W.M.Noble, 'Calender of Huntingdonshire Wills', British Record Society (1911)

J.Norden, Speculi Britanniae (Northants) (1720)

M.Norris, Monumental Brasses, The Craft (1978)

M.Norris, Monumental Brasses, The Memorials (1977)

M.Norris and M.Kellett, Your Book of Brasses (1974)

Norris Library and Museum, St Ives: Collections by Inskip Ladds; John Cole; J.Clements (copy); H.Norris

Northamptonshire Notes and Queries

Northamptonshire Record Office: Hartshorne Collection

Notes and Queries, VIII

Oxford Journal of Monumental Brasses

J.C.Page-Phillips, Macklin's Monumental Brasses (1969)

J.C.Page-Phillips, Palimpsests, The Backs of Monumental Brasses (1980)

F.A.Paley, Notes of 20 Parish Churches in the Five Mile Circle around Peterborough (1859)

J.W.Papworth, Ordinary of British Armorials (1874)

Peterborough Museum and Art Gallery

Peterborough Natural History, Scientific and Archaeological Society Transactions

W.Pinnock, The History and Topography of Huntingdonshire (1822)

J.A.Rastis, Warboys (1974)

Records of Huntingdonshire

Royal Commission on Historical Monuments, Huntingdonshire (1926)

J.P.Rylands, 'Some Memorials of the Family of Ferrar of Little Gidding, Co. Huntingdon', Genealogist N.S.XXVI (1910)

St.Albans Architectural and Archaeological Society Transactions

J.Simpson, A List of the Sepulchral Brasses of England (1857)

Society of Antiquaries collection of rubbings and manuscript 836

Society of Antiquaries Proceedings

M.Stephenson, A List of the Monumental Brasses in

Topographer and Genealogist

Victoria County Histories, Huntingdonshire (1932); Northamptonshire (1906)

H.G.Watson, A History of the Parish of Great Staughton (1916)

J.B.Whitmore, A Genealogical Guide (1953)

R.F.Whistler, The History of Elton (1892)

Topographer and Genealogist

Victoria County Histories, Huntingdonshire (1932); Northamptonshire (1906)

H.G.Watson, A History of the Parish of Great Staughton (1916)

J.B.Whitmore, A Genealogical Guide (1953)

R.F.Whistler, The History of Elton (1892)

Brown Willis, A Survey of the Cathedrals of Lincoln, Ely and Peterborough (1727-30)

Alconbury (1)

°THOMAS COWCHE GENT WAS
BAPTIZED IANVARYE THE 2 6
1 5 8 3 AND HIS BODY LYETH HERE
INTERRED WHO DEPARTED THIS
LIFE VPPON THE 2 0 DAY OF
FEBRVARY 1 6 4 1 ÆTATIS SVÆ 5 8

Abbots Ripton (1)

TO·THE·GLORY·OF·GOD·AMEN.

THE ENTIRE BASE OF THIS TOWER
WAS REBUILT, THE BELL CHAMBER
AND SPIRE MEANTIME REMAINING.
A·D·1877.

EWAN CHRISTIAN.   R. CONWAY. VICAR.
ARCHITECT   L. NEWTON CHURCH·WARDEN'S.
THOˢ WILLIAMS. BUILDER.   G.J. RUST.

Alconbury (2)

SARAH DAUGHTER
OF D. GEORGE REYNOLDS
OCT. 19. 1726

Buckden (1)

Barnack (1)   Barnack (1)

Broughton (1)   Broughton (2)

Broughton (1)

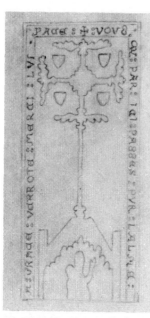

Buckworth (1)

Bythorne (3)

Beneath this stone are deposited the remains of
Philip Hullwait, a native of Bythorne,
who, in the 66th year of his age,
departed this transitory life, Feb. 12, 1788
at Tempsford in the county of Bedford
in hope, through the divine mercy, of a resurrection
to life and felicity eternal.

We know that if our earthly house of this tabernacle
were dissolved, we have a building of God an house
not made with hands, eternal in the Heavens. 1. Cor. V. I.

HEREUNETH BODY OF
SILINA PARRIS Y WIFE
OF WILLIAM PARRIS SHEE
DYED Y 31 OF OCTO 1658

Bythorne (1)

Conington (1)

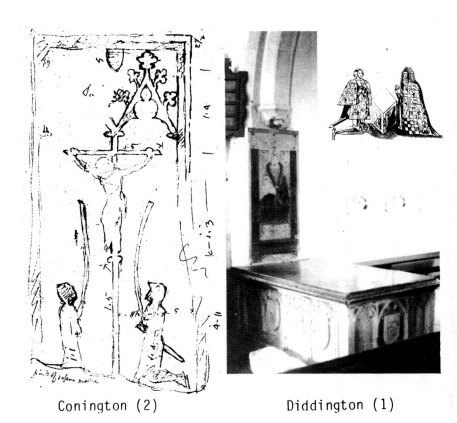

Conington (2) Diddington (1)

Diddington (1)

Diddington (2)

Eaton Socon (1)

Eaton Socon (3)

Eaton Socon (4)   Eaton Socon (4)

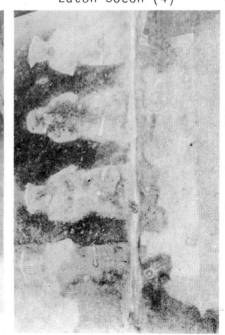

Elton (1)

Eynesbury (2)

Eynesbury (4)

Fenstanton (1)

Godmanchester (1)

Great Gransden (1)

Great Gransden Church Plan

Great Gransden (3)

Great Staughton (5)

Great Stukeley (1)

Hemingford Abbots (1)

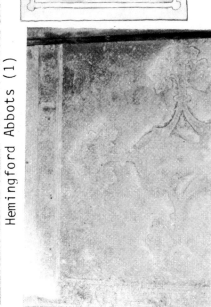

Helpstone (1)

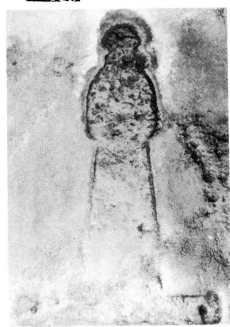

Huntingdon All Saints (1)

Keystone (1)

Leighton Bromswold (1)

Long Stow (1)

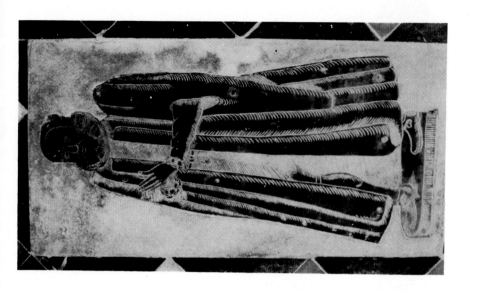

Little Stukeley (1)

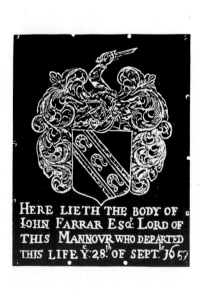

HERE LIETH THE BODY OF
IOHN FARRAR ESQ: LORD OF
THIS MANNOVR WHO DEPARTED
THIS LIFE Y: 28.th OF SEPT.br 1657

Little Gidding (2)

Little Gidding (2)

HERE LYETH Y BODY OF MARY
MAPLETOFT ELDEST DAVGHTER OF SOL
OMON MAPLETOFT & IVDETH HIS WIFE &
GRANDCHILD TO IOHN AND SVSANNA
COLLET SHE DIED Y 14 OF IVLY 1656

Little Gidding (1)

HERE ALSO SLEEPETH SVSAÑA
WIFE TO IOHN COLLET ESQ
BY WHOM SHE HAD ISSVE 8 SONNS
& 8 DAVGHTERS SHE WAS Y ONLY
DAVGHTER OF M NICOLAS FARRAR
OF LONDON MERCHANT & SISTER TO
IOHN FARRER ESQ LATE L OF THIS MANOR
WHO DIED Y 9 OCT 1657 AGED 76 YEARS

Little Gidding (3)

Here lyeth the Body of
Anny Wife of Iohn Ferrar
Esq who departed this life
the 8th of March 1702
She was the Daughter of
Sr Tho. Brook

Little Gidding (4)

Here sleepeth Eleanor Goddard
Daughter to George Long of
London Merchant and Relict
of Iames Goddard of Marston
in Wilts, Gent. who died April
the 20th 1717.

Little Gidding (5)

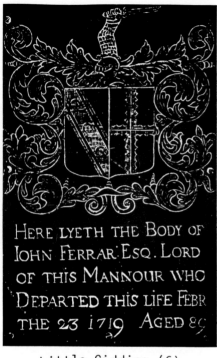

HERE LYETH THE BODY OF
IOHN FERRAR ESQ. LORD
OF THIS MANNOUR WHO
DEPARTED THIS LIFE FEBR
THE 23 1719 AGED 89

Little Gidding (6)

Marholm (1)

Marholm (1)

Marholm (2)

Marholm (1)

Maxey (1)

Maxey (2)

Molesworth (1)

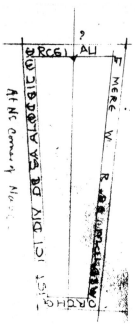

Molesworth (2)

Offord D'Arcy (1)

Offord D'Arcy (2)

Orton Waterville (1)

Offord D'Arcy (1)

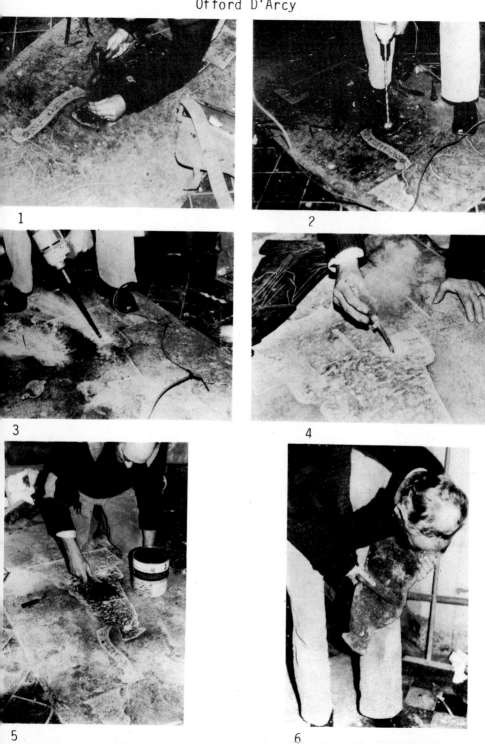

1

2

3

4

5

6

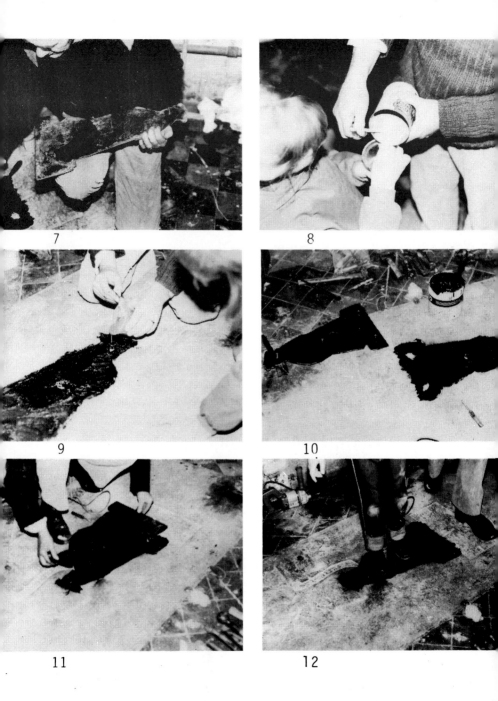

7

8

9

10

11

12

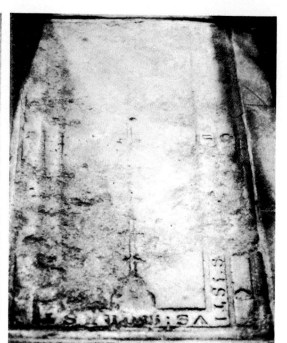

Peterborough Cathedral (1)

Peterborough Cathedral (2)

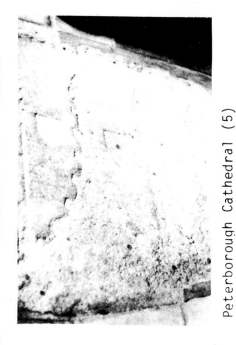

Peterborough Cathedral (5)

Peterborough Cathedral (5)

Peterborough Cathedral (3)

Peterborough Cathedral (3)

Peterborough Cathedral (4)

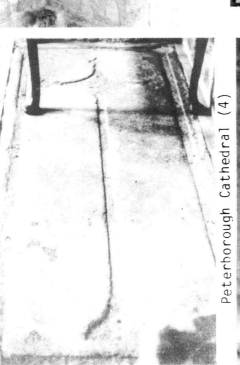

Peterborough Cathedral (6)

Peterborough Cathedral (14)

Peterborough Cathedral (15)

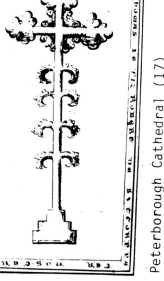

Peterborough Cathedral (16)

Peterborough Cathedral (17)

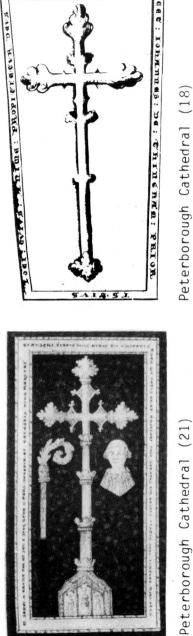

Peterborough Cathedral (18)

Peterborough Cathedral (21)

Peterborough Cathedral (19)

Peterborough Cathedral (23)

Peterborough Cathedral (24)

Peterborough Cathedral (27)

Peterborough Cathedral (30)

Peterborough Cathedral (36)

Peterborough Cathedral (38)

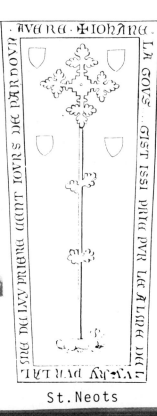

St.Neots

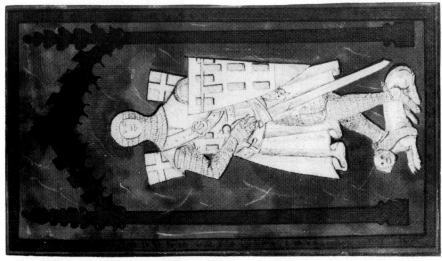

Peterborough Cathedral (20)

Peterborough Cathedral (28)

Peterborough Museum (1)

Peterborough Museum (2)

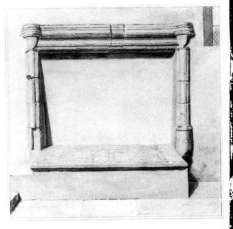

Sawtry (1)

THE MEMORY OF THE IVST IS BLESSED 10 PR:
HERE RESTETH Y BODY OF MARY NEWTON,
Y LATE FAITHFVLL WIFE OF IOHN NEWTON
RECTOR OF THIS CHVRCH, WHO IN THE 32.
YEAR OF HER AGE, ON Y 6 OF AVGVST IN Y
YEAR OF O LORD GOD 1633 DEPARTED
THIS LIFE IN Y TRVE FAYTH OF CHRIST
IN MVCH PACIENCE & COMFORT:
I AM DEAD & MY LIFE IS HID WITH CHRIST
IN GOD WHEN CHRIST WHO IS MY LIFE SHALL
APPEARE THEN SHALL I ALSO APPEARE
VITH HIM IN GLORY.

Sawtry (2)

Sawtry (1)

Somersham (1)

Stanground (1)

Stanground (2)

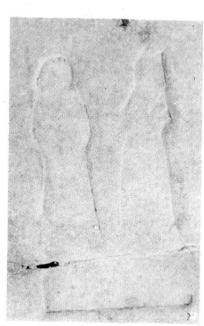

Steeple Gidding (1)

HERE LYETH BVRIED THE BODIES OF RICHARD CVRTHOYS
LATE OF STILTON YEOMAN AND ANNE HIS WIFE BY
WHOM SHE HAD ISSVE THREE SONES THREE DAVGHTERS
IOHN THO: WILLIAM ANN ISABELL AND IOANE
SAID RICHARD DECEASED THE I DAY OF IANVARY
1671 AND THE SAID ANN Y SECOND
OF DECEMB: ANNO 1606

HERE ALSO LYETH BVRIED TH BODIES OF THOMAS
IOHN SONNES OF THE ABOVESAID RICHARD AND ANN
WHICH THOMAS DECEASED THE XVIII DAY OF MAY
ANNO DOMINI 1618 AND IOHN THE XXII OF IVLY
1613 TO WHOSE PIOVS MEMORIE WILLIAM
HIS BROTHER CAVSED THIS MONVMENT
TO BE LAID DOWN

Stilton (1)

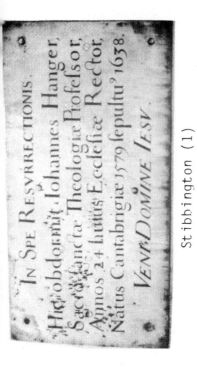

Stibbington (1)

Thornhaugh (1)

Tilbrook (2)

Ufford (1)

Tilbrook (1)

Upwood (1)

Upwood (2)

HERE·LYETH·THE·BODY·OF·EDWARD·COLLINS
THE·SON·OF·EDWARD·COLLIN·OF·WINWICK·YN
·WHO·DEPARTED·THIS·LIFE·THE·28·DAY·OF·IA..
I685·IN·THE·49·YEAR·OF·HIS·AGE·AND·H.
·.SSVE·EDMVND·HIS·ONLY·CHILD.

Winwick (1)

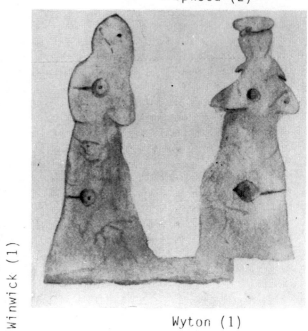

Wyton (1)